# THE OHIO AND MALTA

# THE OHIO AND MALTA

## THE LEGENDARY TANKER THAT REFUSED TO DIE

by

## MICHAEL PEARSON

LEO COOPER

First published in Great Britain 2004 by
LEO COOPER
an imprint of Pen & Sword Books Ltd
47 Church Street,
Barnsley,
South Yorkshire, S70 2AS

Copyright © Michael Pearson, 2004

ISBN 1 84415 031 3

A catalogue record for this book is available
from the British Library

Typeset in Plantin by
Phoenix Typesetting, Auldgirth, Dumfriesshire

Printed in England by
CPI UK.

# Contents

# Acknowledgements

I would like to take this opportunity to express my appreciation to the following persons and organisations for their invaluable assistance in the preparation of this book:

Stato Maggiore della Aeronautica, Rome.

Bundesarchiv, Germany, (researcher Dr Ekkehart Guth).

Mrs Patricia Davis.

Lieutenant Keith Frost, *Ledbury*.

John C. Harper, Historian, Chevron Texaco Archives, San Ramon, California, USA.

Dave Helyar, Merchant Navy Association.

Imperial War Museum Photographic Archive, London.

Stato Maggiore della Marina, Rome.

Ray Morton, *Ohio*.

Danny Omara, *Brisbane Star*.

Norman Warden Owen, *Deucalion*.

Phillip Perry, *Empire Hope*.

The Public Record Office, London.

Allan Shaw, *Ohio*.

Shell Information Technology International Ltd., London, Senior Information Consultant Mrs Veronica Davies.

Vic Simmons, *Rodney*.

Mike Taylor, for once again wading through drafts and proofs and weeding out mistakes!

Mr & Mrs Nigel Welby.

The World Ship Society

To all, my sincere and grateful thanks.

Michael Pearson

# Maps and Diagrams

# Introduction

The first inhabitants of the Maltese archipelago are believed to have been Neolithic settlers who crossed over from nearby Sicily in around 5000 BC. Civilisation flourished in the islands, as elsewhere in the Mediterranean Basin and the Middle East, and is evidenced by the Ggantija Temples, which date back to 3600 – 3200 BC and are believed to be among the oldest man-made structures in the world. In 60 AD Saint Paul of Tarsus was shipwrecked on Malta while being taken as a prisoner to Rome. During his stay he converted many in the islands to Christianity and appointed the first bishop of Malta, St Publius.

The strategic significance of the islands was appreciated from the earliest times, and in their turbulent history they have been occupied by the Phoenicians, Carthaginians, Romans, Arabs, Normans, Spanish, French, British, and perhaps most famously, by the Knights Hospitalers, the Order of St John of Jerusalem, given the islands 'in perpetuity' by Emperor Charles V of Spain in 1530.

In July 1551, Ottoman Turks attacked Gozo, the northernmost island of the group, taking the entire population of 5,000 into slavery in Libya. In July 1565, the Turks returned to lay siege to Malta with a fleet of 181 ships and an army of 30,000 men, the defenders numbering some 600/700 Knights and between 8,000 and 9,000 men. A series of bloody battles ensued, until the Turks were forced to withdraw two months later. In 1566 work commenced on a new fortified capital city, present day Valetta, named for la Valette, commander of the Knights during the Great Siege.

Britain's long association with the islands began in 1798 when Napoleon Bonaparte, en route to Egypt with an army of 54,000 troops, stopped off at Malta. Appreciating the strategic significance of the islands, and the superb Grand Harbour, Bonaparte gave the Knights Hospitalers three days to leave and installed a French Governor with a garrison of 4,000 men. French plans for an empire that stretched as far as India were effectively wrecked by Nelson's destruction of the French fleet at Aboukir Bay, and in 1800 the Maltese rose up in revolt against Bonaparte's garrison. Nelson appointed Captain Alexander Ball to take charge of the blockade, and later arranged for reinforcement of the Maltese insurgents by Portuguese marines and 1,500 British troops. With the French garrison finally starved into surrender, the Maltese, who preferred to remain under British protection, rejected proposals for the return of the Knights Hospitalers, and Malta was confirmed as a British Crown Colony by the Treaty of Paris in 1814.

Of all the tests of stamina and determination to which the population of Malta has been subjected during its long history, perhaps the most stern, perhaps Malta's own 'finest hour', began in June 1940 and continued for almost three years, until May 1943. During the course of this second Great Siege, the civilian population suffered considerably, as Malta was subjected to naval blockade and became one of the most bombed areas in the world, as illustrated by the fact that from 1 January 1942 to 24 July 1942 there existed just one twenty-four-hour period when no bombs fell[1]. Civilians resorted to a life carried on largely underground, retreating to existing caves in the rocks, and digging new ones. Health inevitably suffered, malnutrition was widespread, scabies common, typhoid a constant threat and the cause of at least one epidemic. Civilian casualties from the bombing alone amounted to 1,493 dead and 3,764 wounded, a large number of whom were children[2].

Strenuous efforts were made to keep the islands supplied, but their isolated position surrounded by Axis strongholds made this an exceptionally difficult undertaking. Of the eighty-six supply ships dispatched singly or in convoy to Malta between August 1940 and August 1942, thirty-one were sunk and many others damaged and/or driven back. In appreciation of the island's sacrifice, and in an effort to maintain morale, in April 1942 George VI awarded Malta the George Cross, and insisted on visiting the island as soon as he was able, which he did as an extension to a tour of Allied forces in North Africa, arriving in Grand Harbour aboard the cruiser *Aurora* on 20

June 1943. The population of Malta appreciated the gesture and, *'considering that they had only been told in the early morning, I don't know where they found the flags and how they had time to decorate the streets – but it was done'³*.

The arrival of ships of the *'Pedestal'* convoy on 15 August 1942 greatly eased the plight of Malta and enabled the islands to hold on, but it did not end the ordeal. German Commander in Chief South, Field Marshal Albert Kesselring, unleashed his bombers again in October in yet another series of massive bombing raids in an effort to bring the islands to their knees. The attempt failed, and following the Eighth Army's victory at El Alamein during October/November 1942, the Axis loss of Libyan airfields at last began to relieve the pressure. On 20 November 1942 the four merchantmen of the *'Stonehenge'* convoy delivered some 35,000 tons of supplies to Malta and effectively raised the siege; twelve days' supply of food remained in Malta at the time.

Malta proved to be a festering thorn in the side of the Axis from the beginning of the Mediterranean and North African campaigns to the end. At various times Grand Admiral Raeder, Field Marshal Kesselring and Field Marshal Rommel all advocated invading the islands and solving the problem once and for all. Perhaps Malta's diminutive proportions went some way towards saving her, since when push came to shove, Hitler, Mussolini, and ultimately Rommel himself, all opted for more grandiose schemes at the expense of the capture of these tiny islands. This, it transpired, would prove to be a strategic miscalculation of some significance.

## Notes

[1]  *THE OXFORD COMPANION TO THE SECOND WORLD WAR,* ed. Ian Dear, The Oxford University Press, p. 713.
[2]  *Ibid.*
[3]  Harold Macmillan, *WAR DIARIES,* quoted in *GEORGE VI,* Patrick Howarth, Hutchinson, 1987, p. 150.

CHAPTER ONE

# CRUCIBLE

## I

'Sleeping or waking, Malta is always in my thoughts'. So said Admiral
Lord Nelson during the Napoleonic wars, and it is not difficult to see
why he deemed this tiny island grouping so important. Almost
one and a half centuries later, with Italy's declaration of war on Britain
and France on 10 June 1940, that importance had diminished not
one jot.

The boot-shaped peninsula of the Italian mainland juts into the
central Mediterranean, with the Italian island of Sicily separated from
the 'toe' of the boot by the narrow Straits of Messina. Sardinia, 180
miles* (333km) north-west of Sicily, further extended the prospects
for Italian control of this vital area. Approximately 100 miles (185km)
to the south-west of Sicily is Cape Bon, the north-eastern tip of what
was then Vichy French-occupied Tunisia, on the North African coast.
It was through this narrow channel that all Allied shipping traversing
the Mediterranean from west to east and vice versa had to pass. The
Italian island of Pantelleria, approximately mid-way between Sicily
and Cape Bon, made the passage exceptionally hazardous. Between
Pantelleria and Sicily transit lay through the Sicilian Channel, and
between Pantelleria and Cape Bon through the Narrows, destined to
become infamous among Allied merchant and naval seamen alike. A
large Italian minefield across the northern coast of Pantelleria further
narrowed the gap. Some 80 miles (148km) to the east of Cape Bon,
60 miles (111km) to the south of Sicily, and dwarfed by its neighbour,
lies Malta.

---

* Nautical miles unless otherwise stated.

Positioned 980 miles (1,815km) from Gibraltar and 820 miles (1,519km) from Alexandria, Malta stood at the crossroads of the convoy routes from west to east, and, crucially for the Axis forces in north Africa, from north to south. Malta had been absorbed into the British Empire in the early 1800s, when the islanders enlisted the help of the Royal Navy in the overthrow of Napoleon's French garrison. However, by the late 1930s neither the British Army nor the Royal Air Force believed the island could be defended against air or sea attack from Sicily should Britain find herself at war with Italy's Fascist regime (a not unlikely prospect in view of Mussolini's evident intentions to expand his 'empire' in North Africa). Despite these gloomy assessments, the Royal Navy determined that the effort should be made, appreciating the benefits that the not inappropriately named Grand Harbour offered. Positioned on the north-east coast of the main island, and, in the 1940s, capable of comfortably accommodating the largest warships afloat, the harbour was of inestimable value in naval terms. If significant sections of the British military establishment felt that Malta could and should be abandoned, the Italian military were fully conscious of its strategic importance, and plans to take the island by force were seriously considered in 1935, 1938, and twice in 1940. That they did not make the attempt while the defences were weak would prove to be a costly error.

The tiny Maltese archipelago comprises three main islands: Malta itself is the largest, while Gozo to the north is separated from Malta by Comino. In the years preceding the war, budget restrictions, exacerbated by years of economic depression, prevented the planned construction of purpose-built submarine pens at Gozo and the maintenance and improvement of the island's airfields. While perhaps understandable given the economic woes of the time, both were to prove expensive 'economies'; nevertheless it should be borne in mind that British naval planners in the 1930s counted (perhaps rather too heavily) on the Mediterranean being controlled by their French allies with their large, powerful modern fleet, and bases in North Africa which greatly reduced the strategic value of Malta. In the event, Mussolini did not make a move until he was sure that France would be defeated by Germany alone, the French in fact signing an armistice twelve days after Italian entry into the war. So rapid had been the fall of France that her fleet was not only quickly out of the reckoning as an ally of the Royal Navy, but might conceivably join the Axis. Malta was once more centre stage as the only friendly base between Gibraltar at the western entrance to the Mediterranean, and Alexandria some

2,000 miles (3,704km) farther east. Should Malta fall to the Axis the Royal Navy would be unable to fight its way through the Mediterranean, and would be obliged to undertake a journey of an extra 15,000 miles, (27,780km), and forty-five days duration in order to reach Suez, Alexandria and British forces in Egypt.

The French collapse created problems on land as well as at sea. Britain and France were colonial allies controlling much of the North African littoral, an exception being the Italian occupation of Libya – a wedge between French-occupied Tunisia and the British in Egypt. In manpower terms France was by far the senior partner, her armistice with Germany leaving a British army of around 40,000 facing some 250,000 Italian troops in Libya plus an estimated 350,000 in East Africa. Freed from the threat of attack from Tunisia and anxious to share in the spoils of war, Mussolini ordered the invasion of Egypt. Despite prodding from Il Duce there was no movement until 13 September 1940, when the Italian Tenth Army under Marshal Rodolfo Graziani began its advance over a distance of 60 miles (111km), then stopped. Initially (and unsurprisingly in view of the numerical strength of the opposition) disposed to a defensive campaign, British Commander-in-Chief General Sir Archibald Wavell, encouraged both by Graziani's lack of aggression and a need to defeat him before turning to the problem of East Africa, ordered his field commander, the much-overlooked General Sir Richard O'Connor, to plan and carry out a five day raid in strength against the Italian positions. Following meticulous planning and husbanding of scarce resources, on 7 December General O'Connor's 'raid' commenced. His 36,000 strong force quickly turned the raid into an Italian rout over a ten-week campaign that pushed Graziani back 500 miles (926km) and destroyed his Tenth Army. The British offensive resulted in the capture of 130,000 prisoners, 400 tanks and 1,290 guns, and overran two major fortifications, including Tobruk, at a cost to O'Connor of 476 killed, 1,225 wounded, and 43 missing[1].

O'Connor knocked at the gates of Tripoli and planned the complete expulsion of the Italians from Libya, but elsewhere in the Mediterranean theatre the balance of power also shifted. Secure in the belief that his overwhelming numerical superiority would overcome the puny British force facing Graziani, on 28 October, a mere seven weeks after his invasion of Egypt, and eight weeks prior to the launching of the O'Connor 'raid', Mussolini utilised the Italian occupation of Albania to launch an invasion of Greece, evidently without any attempt to inform Berlin. Determined resistance by Greek forces pushed the invaders back into Albania by 6 December, and, losing patience with his Italian allies, Hitler launched his own invasion of Greece from Bulgaria. In London Prime Minister Churchill decided, against military advice, that the Balkans, not North Africa, constituted the main threat and in February 1941 halted O'Connor's advance and had that General's superb army disbanded and sent to Greece. In the meantime, however, faced by invaders on two fronts, Greek resistance collapsed and the British Expeditionary Force arrived just in time to be withdrawn to Crete, and the disastrous loss of ships and men which ultimately that was to entail.

By the end of January the British advance in Libya stalled, and on 11 February troops of the German 5th Light Division landed at Tripoli, to be followed two days later by their commanding officer, Lieutenant General Erwin Rommel. Having come so close to taking Libya, British forces now faced one of Germany's most capable generals (one who would adopt O'Connor's tactics with equally successful results), and a two year see-saw campaign in the western desert, a campaign in which Malta was destined to play a decisive role.

★　★　★　★

A significant similarity existed between the economies of Britain, Germany and Italy in 1940, a similarity of crucial importance for modern mechanised warfare, and an underlying reason for the struggle in North Africa. Not one of these principal players in the Mediterranean drama about to unfold had an indigenous oil supply with which to keep their voracious armed forces on the move.

During his initial term as First Lord of the Admiralty, Winston Churchill had, in the early 1900s, determined that the fuel for Britain's fleet should move from coal to oil, and obtained government backing for millionaire adventurer and explorer William Knox-Darcy to prospect vast tracts of Persia (now Iran). Knox-Darcy searched for seven years at the cost of most of his fortune, but eventually discovered huge deposits of oil. The Anglo-Persian Oil Company (later to become BP) came into being, and the British government took a controlling interest. The precious black gold would necessarily require transportation either through the Suez Canal or, in the event that the Mediterranean was to be denied to British shipping, by the much longer route around the Cape of Good Hope.

While having no oil as such, Germany had deposits of oil shale from which it was possible to synthesize oil: 2,200,000 tons (2,235,200

4

tonnes) in 1939, rising to a peak of 5,700,000 tons (5,791,200 tonnes) in 1943[2]. This fell considerably short of Germany's needs however, and Rumania found herself badgered into joining the Axis for her oil. Supplies, nevertheless, remained a constant problem throughout the war, and led to determined German efforts to capture Russian oilfields in the Caucasus.

With no oil of any kind, Italy fared worst of all, and up to 1943 had to import all her oil requirements from Germany or Rumania. In view of Germany's own shortfall, Hitler ensured first call on Rumanian supplies; consequently Italy was often reduced to desperate measures, on more than one occasion having to pump oil from her battleships in order to fuel merchantmen for supply convoys to North Africa.

★   ★   ★   ★

In view of Malta's susceptibility to air attack from Sicily, Britain established her main naval base in the Mediterranean at Alexandria, thanks in large measure to Winston Churchill, who forcefully vetoed an Admiralty proposal to bring the fleet west and abandon the Eastern Mediterranean altogether[3]. In addition, Gibraltar saw the arrival of Force H for operations in the Mediterranean or the Atlantic as opportunities presented themselves, or circumstances dictated.

Finding that the Royal Navy would have to maintain control of the Mediterranean without assistance from France, attention soon focused on Malta. Churchill, in his memo of 12 July 1940 to General Sir Hastings Ismay\*, urged the reinforcement of air defences '*in the strongest manner*'[4], to enable use of Grand Harbour by units of the Fleet as a stage in the development of the island for offensive operations.

In order to realise the island's full potential, much work would be required to bring the three aerodromes and other military installations to full operational condition. However, the Italian *Commando Supremo* had no intention of allowing Malta to be developed as a military base and imposed an immediate naval blockade. To emphasise Italy's intentions, within twenty-four hours of Mussolini's declaration of war, Malta had suffered its first air raid. This was nevertheless an early indication of why this tiny island group would prove to be such a problem for the Axis as, in its attempts to neutralise the British bases,

---

\* Churchill's Chief of Staff and liaison with the Chiefs of Staff Committee, in the Prime Minister's dual role as Minister of Defence.

some 200 front-line aircraft, which otherwise would almost certainly have supported Marshal Graziani in Libya, were diverted to Sicily. The Luftwaffe would face the same problem later in the war.

Although considered too risky as a permanent base for large fleet units, the naval dockyards in Malta, with their well equipped service and repair facilities, were maintained, and a submarine base established at Manoel Island in Lazaretto Creek just along the coast from Grand Harbour and the capital, Valetta. From September 1940, submarines of the specially formed Tenth Submarine Flotilla arrived on station, and aircraft numbers also started to rise – fighters for the RAF bases at Hal Far and Takali, bombers for Luqa. Despite its reservations and given the decision to hold the islands, the Army steadily increased its presence, until by 1942 some 30,000 infantry were stationed there, including two troops of tanks. Approximately one-third of all Army personnel were Maltese, plus many hundreds, possibly thousands, of islanders serving with the Navy and at the airfields[5].

As 1940 gave way to 1941, attacks on Axis supply convoys in the Mediterranean began to have an impact. As a result, to bolster the *Regia Aeronautica*, in January 1941 Hitler transferred Luftflotte X to Italy, with many units being stationed in Sicily specifically to counter the threat from Malta. These reinforcements had the desired effect and air superiority over Malta was in danger of being wrested from the RAF. However, by May 1941, Luftflotte X found itself transferred to Greece to support the German invasion of Crete, and thence farther east to support *Operation Barbarossa,* Hitler's invasion of Russia, commencing June 1941. The effects on Axis convoys to Rommel in North Africa were immediately noticeable: 125,000 tons (127,000 tonnes) of supplies delivered to Libya in June fell to 50,706 tons (51,577 tonnes) in July, which included only 12,000 tons (12,192 tonnes) of petrol, a massive 41 per cent of this vital commodity being lost en route[6]. So wary did the Axis become of Malta that quantities of supplies, instead of taking the shorter convoy route around Sicily to Tripoli, were sent along the coast of Greece and into the eastern Mediterranean (see map page 154). Having this measure forced upon them drastically cut tonnage movable by the Italians, as voyage times were much longer and all available shipping had already been pressed into service. Between 1 June and 31 October 1941, some 220,000 tons (223,520 tonnes) of Axis shipping were sunk on the convoy routes from Italy to Libya, of which Malta's RAF and Fleet Air Arm squadrons accounted for an estimated 86,250 tons (87,630 tonnes)[7]

– to which must be added losses inflicted by Malta's submarines and other naval vessels, bringing the island fortress' contribution to over half the total. One reason for this impressive strike-rate was Allied air reconnaissance which, from Egypt, could only pick up enemy convoys well into their voyage and therefore closer to their destination, whereas reconnaissance from Malta could pinpoint them shortly after departure from Italy, allowing air/sea strikes to be despatched correspondingly sooner. *Ultra* decrypts would also give early warning of convoy movements, although a reconnaissance flight would still need to be sent to hide the fact that code breakers at Bletchley Park were reading Axis radio traffic.

★   ★   ★   ★

Having significantly strengthened Malta's defences, particularly in respect of anti-aircraft weaponry and fighter aircraft, the decision was taken to risk basing a force of warships there, Churchill's directive of 14 April 1941 stating that:

> . . . *in order to control the sea communications across the Mediterranean, sufficient suitable naval forces must be based on Malta, and protection must be afforded to these naval forces by the Air Force at Malta, which must be kept at the highest strength in fighters . . . that the Malta aerodromes can contain . . .*[8]

Such was the pressure for ships under which the Royal Navy operated in its worldwide role, that it was not until 21 October that Force K, comprising the light cruisers *Aurora* (Flagship, Senior Officer Captain W.A. Agnew), and *Penelope**, plus supporting destroyers *Lance* and *Lively*, arrived in Grand Harbour. Delayed they may have been, but they arrived just in time to participate in spectacular fashion in one of Malta's most successful periods of offensive operations.

General Rommel's dazzling brand of mobile warfare quickly drove weakened British forces back towards the Egyptian border (although he was as yet unable to capture Tobruk), and in succeeding months, as the British initially rushed reinforcements to the area then tried desperately to recover the position, he defeated two major counter-offensives. It was, however, the drastic reduction in supplies to the combined Italian-German Panzer Armee resulting from the

* 'Arethusa' class 6 x 6" (152mm) main armament.

withdrawal of Luftflotte X that enabled the British Western Desert Force, now designated the Eighth Army and under the command of General Alan Cunningham, to launch *Operation Crusader* on 18 November 1941, in the process of beating Rommel to the punch, that general's own plans for another offensive being well advanced.

To supply the impending Axis campaign, a large convoy comprising five freighters and two tankers sailed eastwards from Naples on 7 November, following which the planned route took it south towards Benghazi and west to Tripoli – a time-consuming dog-leg that virtually doubled the distance compared with the route from Sicily down the Tunisian coast. A close escort of six destroyers was provided plus an additional screen comprising the heavy cruisers *Trieste* and *Trento*<sup>*</sup> with a further four destroyers. Force K was therefore heavily outgunned, but had one priceless advantage – radar. A Malta-based RAF reconnaissance aircraft picked up the convoy on the afternoon of 8 November en route to the Greek coast and, as evening twilight faded into night, Force K put to sea to intercept.

It looked initially as if the British squadron might miss the convoy during the night, but blips appeared on radar screens followed by visual sightings, and Captain Agnew formed his ships into line astern the flagship – *Aurora, Lance, Penelope, Lively* – and closed the targets at high speed. Without radar, convoy and escort were taken completely by surprise, and in the ensuing engagement all seven merchantmen plus three Italian destroyers were sunk. Force K emerged undamaged.

Submarines and aircraft from Malta and Egypt also inflicted serious losses on Rommel's supply convoys, and of the 79,208 tons (80,475 tonnes) of equipment and petrol despatched during November 1941, only 29,843 tons (30,320 tonnes) arrived – a staggering loss rate of 62 per cent. In fact the only petrol to reach Axis troops in North Africa had to be taken in cans aboard cruisers, and amounted to a meagre 2,471 tons (2,510 tonnes)[9].

Had it been possible to maintain this strike rate, Rommel's Italian–German Panzer Armee must have been plunged into crisis by early 1942, but the pendulum had already begun to swing back, and a series of disasters awaited the Royal Navy in the Mediterranean theatre which would make the role of Malta, the 'unsinkable aircraft carrier', ever more pivotal.

On 13 November, *U81* torpedoed and sank the aircraft carrier *Ark*

* 'Trento' class 8 x 8" (203mm) main armament.

8

*Royal* off Gibraltar; on 15 November, *U557* torpedoed and sank the light cruiser *Galatea* off Alexandria; and on 25 November, *U331* torpedoed and sank the battleship *Barham* 60 miles (111km) north of Sollum. However the most daring, and certainly the most spectacular, strike against the British Mediterranean fleet occurred on the night of 17 December when six Italian frogmen aboard two-man 'human torpedoes' despatched from the submarine *Scire*, penetrated the defences at Alexandria and mined the battleships *Valiant* and *Queen Elizabeth*. All six frogmen were captured but both ships (the only serviceable British battleships then in the Mediterranean) were sunk. Fortunately, Alexandria harbour is comparatively shallow and the ships were later refloated and repaired, but both were out of action for an extensive period.

To cap this catalogue of disasters, a much-strengthened Force K strayed into a minefield off Tripoli on the night of 18/19 November, resulting in the sinking of the cruiser *Neptune* and destroyer *Kandahar*, and damage to the cruisers *Aurora* and *Penelope*. In North Africa, *Operation Crusader* pushed the Afrika Korps back, but General Sir Neil Ritchie replaced an exhausted Cunningham, and Rommel, the Desert Fox, already planned his next offensive.

★　★　★　★

Stung by crippling supply losses to North Africa in November 1941, Hitler appointed the energetic and skilful Field Marshal Albert Kesselring Commander-in-Chief of German forces in the Mediterranean theatre, although in a complicated anomaly Rommel remained – nominally at any event, since he tended to go his own way – subordinate to Italian Marshal Bastico, who was in turn responsible to *Commando Supremo* and Mussolini. At a briefing in Berlin, Hitler stressed that Kesselring's prime mission would be to neutralise Malta, and to assist him with his task Luftflotte II would, with the onset of the Russian winter, be transferred from the Russian front to Sicily. Once again forces urgently required elsewhere were to be used in an attempt to crush the islands. Without Malta, the powerful Luftflotte II would almost certainly have reinforced Rommel, at that time being driven back by *Crusader*.

A pilot himself, Kesselring transferred from the army to the then fledgling Luftwaffe in 1935, briefly occupying the post of Chief of Staff in 1936. Consequently, with experience of both arms he knew what was and was not possible with air power alone. This, coupled with a sound grasp of strategy, prompted him to suggest doing the job properly by occupying the islands. Hitler brushed the suggestion aside, and as Kesselring was not yet fully 'in the picture' he did not press the point, although he would have cause to return to it later.[10]

# II

The Mediterranean theatre held a clear advantage in men and matériel for the Axis in the early years of the war. Accordingly the invasion and occupation of Malta should have been well within their capabilities – yet time and again opportunities were wasted. From the outset, German naval C-in-C Grand Admiral Erich Raeder urged that Britain should be defeated before any invasion of Russia, and believing the Mediterranean to be a main artery of empire, stressed the neutralisation of British bases at Gibraltar, Malta, and Suez. Not being one of Hitler's inner circle of confidants, Raeder may not have been aware of, or chose to ignore, the racial and ideological motives inherent in Hitler's designs on Russia, but in purely military terms his ideas deserved a better hearing than they received.

On his arrival in Italy on 28 November 1941, Field Marshal Kesselring made it a priority to undertake a tour of his command area from Sicily to North Africa. The tour was to ' . . . *confirm my view that the menace to our communications from Malta must be removed'.*[11] As facilities in Sicily were not immediately able to accommodate the massive reinforcement of hundreds of additional Luftwaffe aircraft to be based there, Kesselring was obliged to make do with what was available and set about that task with typical energy. By early December regular attacks by between sixty and seventy Axis aircraft per week were under way, rising to 200 and more by the end of the month; but, inspired by Air Officer Commanding, Air Vice Marshal Hugh P. Lloyd, the RAF kept their outdated, pitifully few (and getting fewer) Hurricane fighters airborne to harry the attacking formations.

Following the November debacle the number of shipments from Italy to North Africa dropped. Nevertheless attacks by bombers, submarines and surface forces from Malta continued despite Kesselring's offensive, and a woefully insufficient total of 39,092 tons (39,717 tonnes) of supplies (including gasoline) were delivered to Rommel in December, at a loss rate of 18 per cent[12] of the total despatched.

The Luftwaffe assault gathered pace during January and February and some 2,000 bomber sorties were flown over the island. An estimated 1,000 tons (1,016 tonnes) of bombs were dropped on the island in February alone[13] – and doubled in March. Conditions in the island were grim, and set to get much worse. Malta was as dependent on supplies from the outside as Rommel, and the combination of increasing air attacks and the naval blockade bit deeply into the island's reserves as the problem of feeding the 270,000 civilian population, plus military personnel, began to assume alarming proportions. On 21 February, Malta's Governor, Lieutenant General Sir William Dobbie, telegraphed the Secretary of State for the Colonies that oil of all kinds had become particularly scarce, rationing was being stepped up, non-essential bus journeys curtailed, and that '. . . *civil consumption of kerosene, after bread the most important commodity for civil use in Malta,** [is] *half its normal level*'[14]. Maintaining food and fuel for the civilian population was of vital importance. Food rationing already threatened to reach crisis point, the general health of the people deteriorated noticeably, scabies was rampant, and summer would see the outbreak of a typhoid epidemic. Asking military personnel to tighten their belts another notch and 'rough it' was one thing, but asking mothers with babies and young children was quite another, and if civilian morale collapsed the islands would become untenable.

Kesselring's objective was not primarily to break down civilian morale, but to destroy Malta as a base for offensive operations, and in this he was undoubtedly succeeding. In January 1942 the 43,328 tons (44,021 tonnes) of supplies and 22,842 tons (23,207 tonnes) of gasoline despatched from Italy reached North Africa without loss, while February and March saw another 66,990 tons (68,062 tonnes) of supplies and 39,563 tons (40,196 tonnes) of fuel discharged for a perfectly acceptable loss of 9 per cent of the total sent.[15] Despite these highly promising developments, Kesselring, from his headquarters in Rome, continued to press for the invasion and capture of the islands while, unknown to him, Grand Admiral Raeder in Berlin campaigned for the same objective. The fly in the ointment, not for the first or last time, was C-in-C Luftwaffe, Reichsmarschall Hermann Goering. Raeder and others in the German High Command pressed for the capture of Malta in April 1941 hard on the heels of the British defeat

---

* For cooking, any natural fuel supply that Malta may have possessed was long since exhausted.

in Greece and the subsequent withdrawal of the British Expeditionary Force to Crete. Raeder believed a German invasion of Crete to be of negligible benefit and that any attempt to withdraw the British troops there would involve the Royal Navy in substantial losses, which, in the event, turned out to be chillingly accurate. The Admiral, supported by General Alfred Jodl, Chief of the Operations Staff of the German High Command, held the invasion of Malta to be a comparatively simple operation, and of infinitely more strategic value. Goering, a Hitler favourite from 'the old days' of the 1930s, demurred, and the invasion of Crete went ahead, successfully, but at such cost to the elite German paratroops that they were never used in that role again.

Called to Führer headquarters in February 1942, Kesselring again stressed the need to remove the Maltese thorn from their side once and for all, while Goering maintained that the island could be reduced by the Luftwaffe alone, as he had boasted that the Allied withdrawal from Dunkirk could be stopped by the Luftwaffe alone, that the Luftwaffe could bomb Britain into submission alone, etc. Tempers flared and the meeting ended with Hitler grasping Kesselring by the arm and telling him to *'Keep your shirt on, Field-Marshal Kesselring. I am going to do it!'*[16]

What made Hitler change his mind at this juncture is open to interpretation. Certainly Rommel, at that time also a Hitler favourite, was for the time being supporting Kesselring and in fact asked for the *'attractive little job'*[17] of taking Malta to be entrusted to his Italian–German Panzer Armee. Additionally Raeder had, during February, presented Hitler with his Grand Plan, a particularly grandiose, but nonetheless impressive, scheme visualising the occupation of Malta as an essential first step to the capture of Egpyt, followed by a joining of forces between the Panzer Armee and German armies forging down through the Russian Caucasus; the combined force pressing on to the Persian Gulf, India, and points East until a link up had been established with their Japanese allies. Whether a physical joining with the Japanese was practical or necessary is debatable. However, if German forces were to gain control of the Suez Canal and Arabian Gulf and forge on into Persia, Britain's oil supplies would be cut and she would be out of the war.

Unsurprisingly, Hitler liked the sound of the Grand Plan.

★   ★   ★   ★

12

For Winston Churchill and the War Cabinet, the Malta problem boiled down to supplies and Spitfires – and how to get both to the islands in quantity. As was becoming the norm, oil was in desperately short supply and in December 1941, C-in-C Mediterranean, Admiral Cunningham, and naval C-in-C Malta, Vice Admiral Wilbraham Ford, combed the British and Commonwealth tanker fleets for a ship fast enough, 15 knots or more, to make the hazardous trip in convoy from Alexandria to Grand Harbour. None could be found and a decision was taken to use the fast cargo liner *Breconshire*, which, during conversion to a naval supply ship, had her deeptank capacity increased to 5,000 tons (5,080 tonnes) – still half the capacity of a good sized tanker, but the best that could be managed given the essential speed requirement. *Breconshire* was to make the trip several times in the coming months and, together with the 40-knot minelayers *Manxman* and *Welshman*, became a vital lifeline for the islands. One or other of the minelayers would make the high-speed dash from Gibraltar alone, loaded to the gunwales with essential foodstuffs and munitions – but these, together with supply trips made by submarine and air transport barely nibbled at the problem. The increasingly urgent need was for re-supply by convoy.

Numerous attempts were made during the first half of 1942, all engaged in with great courage in the face of phenomenal air and sea attack. Most merchantmen that made the attempt were either driven back or sent to the bottom, although from time to time a battered freighter or two would be fought through to Grand Harbour – but no tankers. On 26 March disaster struck when *Breconshire* was bombed and sunk in Grand Harbour.

By April, Kesselring was able to hurl some 600 Luftwaffe and *Regia Aeronautica* aircraft against Malta, to be met by twenty to thirty serviceable RAF fighters[18]. Raids came in around the clock with aerodromes and other military installations bombed three to four times a day and many attacks lasting for hours at a time. During the course of this harrowing month for the islanders, 6,700 tons (6,807 tonnes) of bombs were dropped – more than the total inflicted on London for the whole of 1940. By now over 10,000 homes were wrecked, 20,000 damaged, and 1,000 civilians killed.[19] For much of the population, life was reduced to the very basics, and comprised a semi-permanent existence in underground shelters or catacombs cut into the very rock of the islands. Still their morale did not break, but Governor Dobbie's entreaties to London mounted, and a decision was taken that he should be 'rested'. General Lord Gort, VC, replaced him, arriving at Kalafrana seaplane base at the southern tip of the islands on 7 May.

Spitfires in small numbers were despatched to Malta from the aircraft carrier HMS *Eagle* during March, but at 4.30am on 27 April, in the largest single reinforcement so far, forty-seven of the much-needed fighters took off from the U.S. carrier *Wasp* and landed later that morning at Luqa and Takali aerodromes. Unfortunately, Axis reconnaissance picked up the reinforcement and by lunchtime the island again endured heavy attack. Some of the new Spitfires got off the ground but most were destroyed where they stood, still being armed and refuelled following their arrival. Such was the pounding inflicted on the island that the Tenth Submarine Flotilla, bomber squadrons and any surface ships remaining, were withdrawn to Egypt. The move would have been inevitable in any event as there was by now very little fuel left with which to keep them in action. To underline the almost total extinction of Malta's offensive capability, April 1942 saw 150,389 tons (152,795 tonnes) of supplies landed by the Axis in North Africa, including a vital 48,031 tons (48,800 tonnes) of fuel[20], with a loss rate of a mere 1 per cent of the total.

In contrast to improving fortunes for the Panzer Armee, Malta's supply position became ever more precarious, underlined by an end of April memo from the Chief of the Imperial General Staff to the Chiefs of Staff Committee and the War Department, giving the estimated date for exhaustion of vital supplies on the islands:

*Food:* Approximate date of exhaustion end June / early July

*White Oils:*

| | |
|---|---|
| Aviation spirit | mid August |
| Benzine | mid June |
| Kerosene | early July |

*Black Oils:*

| | |
|---|---|
| Submarine diesel | early May |
| Naval fuel oil | on fuelling of current ships in dock |
| Fuel for generating station | early June[21] |

The figures for oil stocks excluded anything that might be extricated from the upturned hull of *Breconshire* in Grand Harbour, but this would take time – another commodity rapidly running out for the islands. If food stocks were to be used up by the end of June, Malta would be forced to surrender weeks before supplies were finally at an end.

By the beginning of May, Rommel's Panzer Armee was not only fully equipped and supplied but there was even a surplus and on 27 May, Rommel commenced an attack which, despite fierce fighting, once again threw the Eighth Army back. Attack and counter-attack followed but Rommel's advance continued and on 21 June Tobruk finally capitulated. Eschewing any delay, the newly promoted Field Marshal Rommel crossed into Egypt on 23 June.

Might Admiral Raeder's Grand Plan work after all? Cairo seemed invitingly close.

At Sidi Barrani on 26 June, the Axis High Command for the Mediterranean theatre came together for a crucial meeting to discuss their next move. Kesselring insisted that, as agreed at the February meeting with Hitler, Malta should now be taken. The ferocity of his air assault had in large measure destroyed the island's defences, and, although Spitfire reinforcements arrived during May, invasion and occupation would now be easier than at any time since 1940. Flushed with victory and promotion, Rommel disagreed and insisted that he be allowed to continue his advance to Cairo, which he expected to fall within ten days. There would be time enough for Malta after his triumphal entry into the Egyptian capital, accompanied by Mussolini, who had arrived in Egypt in anticipation of the great event. The decision was referred to Hitler, who had by now also cooled toward the invasion of Malta, codenamed 'Herkules'. To General Kurt Student, scheduled to command the advance attack by German and Italian paratroops, he commented:

> The formation of a bridgehead via your airborne troops is guaranteed. But . . . once the attack has been started . . . the British Alexandria and Gibraltar squadrons will of course immediately run an approach. You will then see the Italian reaction . . . everything will return to the harbours . . . warships as well as cargo ships . . . and you will sit alone on the island with your paratroops[22].

Hitler backed Rommel and the advance into Egypt continued, but the Eighth Army, with General Sir Claude Auchinleck replacing Sir Neil Ritchie in command, dug in at El Alamein and refused to budge. Taunted by the minarets of Cairo, Rommel continued his assault – his urgent need for reinforcement drawing in troops designated for the Malta invasion force. To further assist with the capture of the

Egyptian capital, Luftwaffe units in Sicily were moved to the Eastern Mediterranean, and while this further reduced the possibility of an Allied convoy from Alexandria to Malta, it did offer the possibility of forcing one through from the west, via Gibraltar.

Replacing General Dobbie with General Gort as governor of the besieged islands had not in any way alleviated the dire supply problem (although Gort himself was not one to add to the difficulties, and was often to be seen pedalling furiously around the streets of Malta on a bicycle, having declined the use of petrol-driven transport), and on 21 June the new governor telegraphed London:

*Present bread ration 10.5 ounces daily.*

*Kerosene for domestic consumption issued every other week instead of weekly.*

*Edible oil to be issued . . . one half pint every 6 weeks.*

*2 issues of sugar to be 'skipped' in July/August.*

*Butter to be absorbed in fats ration to last longer.*

*All brewing to stop.*[23]

At the same time, Gort proposed the requisitioning of the island's wheat and barley crop, and the slaughter of most of the pigs, sheep, cows, goats and poultry, expressing the hope that with these measures the islands might hold out until September, but continuing '. . . *you will realise that we shall from now onwards live a hand to mouth existence until such time as a convoy can reach us*'.

The response from Whitehall was to agree to these proposals, with the exception of the slaughter of animals, which was felt to be unnecessary and would cause resentment among farmers. Gort patiently replied that the only fodder left on the islands comprised 900 tons (914 tonnes) of oats and 200 tons (203 tonnes) of meal and cake. With the oats required for horses, essential as draft animals given the severe petrol shortages, farm animals would die of starvation if they were not slaughtered. Farmers would be offered 'good prices' by way of compensation. Between bombs and starvation, living long enough to collect must have seemed a less than certain prospect.

# Notes

1   *THE DESERT GENERALS*, Corelli Barnett, Wm. Kimber & Co., second edition, September 1960, p. 62.

2   *THE OXFORD COMPANION TO THE SECOND WORLD WAR*, ed. Ian Dear, p. 459.

3   When, later in the war, this proposal again reared its head due to increased air attacks on Alexandria, Churchill again vetoed the move, dryly observing that His Majesty's ships must from time to time come under fire –that is what they are for!

4   *PRO.CAB 120/624.*

5   *SUPREME GALLANTRY*, Malta's Role in the Allied Victory 1939-1945, Tony Spooner, John Murray (Publishers) Ltd., 1996, p. 10.

6   *THE ITALIAN NAVY IN WORLD WAR II*, Commander Marc' Antonio Bragadin, United States Naval Institute, 1957, p. 132.

7   *THE RIGHT OF THE LINE*, John Terraine, Wordsworth Editions Ltd., 1997, p. 353.

8   *Op.cit.* (note 4).

9   *Op.cit.* (note 6), p. 141.

10  *THE MEMOIRS OF FIELD MARSHAL KESSELRING,* Purnell Book Services, 1974, pp. 104/105.

11  *Ibid.* p. 109.

12  *Op. cit.* (note 6), p. 154.

13  *THE AIR BATTLE FOR MALTA*, James Douglas-Hamilton, The Diaries of a Spitfire Pilot, Airlife Publishing Ltd., 2000, p.17.

14  *PRO.AIR/2428.*

15  *Op.cit.* (note 6), p. 154.

16  *Op.cit.* (note 10), p. 109.

17  *ROMMEL IN HIS OWN WORDS*, ed. Dr. John Pimlott, Greenhill Books, Lionel Leventhal Ltd., 1994, p. 95.

18  *Op.cit.* (note 13), p. 20.

19  *Ibid.* p. 19.

20  *Op.cit.* (note 6), p. 155.

21  *Op.cit.* (note 14).

22  *THE GREAT ENCYCLOPEDIA OF THE SECOND WORLD WAR*, C. Zentner, Munich 1988, p. 359.

23  *PRO.CAB 120/622.*

# CHAPTER TWO

# THROUGH A GLASS, DARKLY

## I

In 1894 oil was discovered in Corsicana, Texas, and in 1897 Joseph Stephen 'Buckskin Joe' Cullinan, a veteran of market leaders Standard Oil and the Pennsylvania oil fields, arrived to advise the bustling oil region how to market the new found 'black gold'. Initially Texas crude came to be regarded as inferior to the Pennsylvania alternative, however, Cullinan energetically worked at developing markets for Corsicana oil, until, in January 1901, news broke of the 'Spindletop' gusher in Beaumont. Within twenty-four hours of the discovery Cullinan arrived in the bustling oil town, and within two months secured enough backing to form the Texas Fuel Company, with authorised capital of $50,000.

Surviving growing pains and a severe fire in the Spindletop oil field, which Cullinan played a leading part in extinguishing, the Texas Fuel Company grew rapidly, in January 1903 acquiring an option on an 865-acre site at nearby Sour Lake for the drilling of three test wells before the expiry of the option in April 1903. Consideration from Texas Fuel to the Sour Lake Spring Company amounted to $1,000,000, despite the fact that nobody on either side of the negotiations had ever seen anything like a million dollars! Texas Fuel had to strike oil in quantity or go under, and fortunately for Cullinan and his partners they did not have long to wait. On 8 January, Well No.3 proved to be a 'gusher'.

The Texas Fuel Company adopted the brand name Texaco, and the five-pointed emblem of its native 'Lone Star' State as a corporate logo. The company purchased its first tanker, the s.s. *Florida*, in 1903, and assets grew from $3,500,000 that same year to $75,000,000 in 1914. Texaco and the star emblem became familiar worldwide.

With pipeline, engineering, and oil exploration projects from Colombia to Saudi Arabia, Texaco came through the financial crises of the 1930s and by 1939 had developed into a major player in the global oil business.

# II

The waters of the Delaware River at Chester, Pennsylvania, were rough, churned by a northeasterly gale. Launching of the big new Texaco tanker was delayed and sage heads in and around the dock-yard agreed that to put back the scheduled launch of the ship was a bad omen – men connected with the sea worldwide are notoriously superstitious. Better, they reasoned, to risk the gale than bad luck.

The following day, 20 April 1940, dawned overcast, grey, and rainy, but the river was calmer and the ship's sponsor, Mrs. Florence E. Rogers, mother of the President of the Texas Company, Mr. W.S.S. Rogers, was at last able to proceed with the launch and naming ceremony of Sun Shipbuilding and Dry Dock Company's Hull No. 190, on Slipway No.2. Mr. Rogers hailed from Columbus, and the family enjoyed considerable status in his native state consequently this first in a new class of five sister ships bore the name *Ohio*.

The new ship was primarily designed for the Texas Company's distribution service around the U.S. coast and the Gulf of Mexico, and consequently a comparatively large number of cargo tanks were incorporated into her design – two longitudinal and twenty-three transverse bulkheads enclosed nine centre tanks, eight large and sixteen smaller wing tanks. This feature created a honeycomb to enable the ship to carry several different grades of oil simultaneously, the numerous tanks being served by a state of the art pumping and pipeline system powered from a pump room abaft the midships super-structure, facilitating the loading and discharge of cargoes without cross-contamination. Combined with a system of longitudinal framing for the deck and the base of the centre tanks, transverse framing to the side shell, and stiffeners on the bulkheads supported by two deep horizontal girders, the honeycomb effect also made the ship immensely strong. With a weather eye on the deteriorating situation across both the Pacific and the Atlantic oceans, the U.S.

19

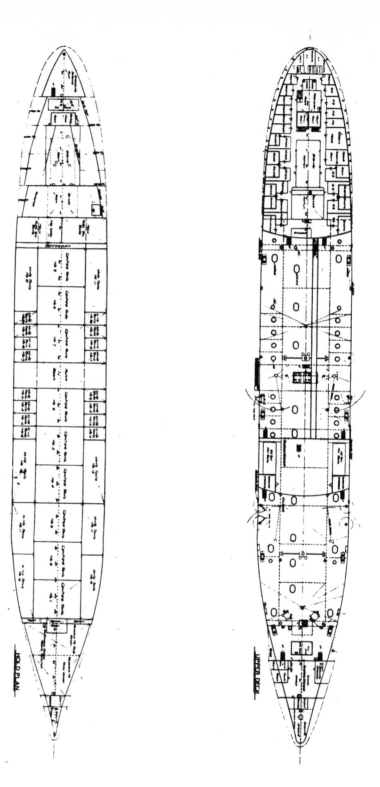

S.S. "OHIO"

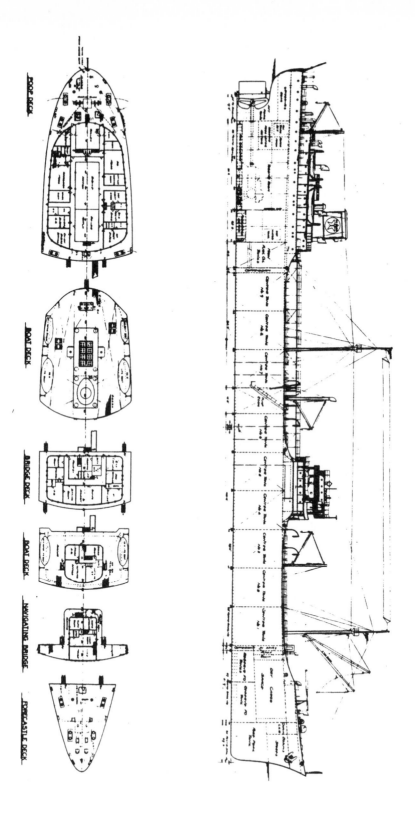

Department of Defense got their heads together with Texaco and agreed a number of design changes which resulted in *Ohio* being, at 14,150 tons deadweight*, the largest tanker yet built, and, with 10,000 SHP Westinghouse steam turbines capable of driving her through the water at 17 knots, the fastest. With an overall length of 513' 10" (156.6m) she was also one of the largest ships of electrically welded construction afloat[1]. Only the side shell, framing, and part of the superstructure were riveted.

Crew facilities and accommodation were all to the highest standards, her crew of forty-one officers and men each having a separate cabin – unheard of at the time. Master and Chief Officer were provided with mahogany-lined cabins amidships, with furniture of solid mahogany. The midship superstructure also contained the wheelhouse, chartroom and radio rooms, plus cabins for deck officers, and a well-appointed dining saloon. Engineer officers were berthed in cabins in a steel house on the poop deck, the chief engineer and first assistant's rooms being finished in mahogany. Petty officers and crew were quartered in cabins on the upper deck, which also housed the crewmen's mess room and a large smoking room. Officers' and petty officers' mess rooms were arranged on the poop deck. To the steel-cutters, shipwrights, welders, riveters and myriad craftsmen at Sun Shipbuilding she was a 'classy' ship. She was also a beautiful ship, from the elegant sweep of her schooner bow, along the graceful lines of her hull to the cruiser stern. The neat, compact superstructure, curved forward and aft, added to her streamlined appearance.

Mid-morning on 18 June, and *Ohio*, now completed and in the livery of her prospective owners – black hull with red boot topping, white superstructure, black funnel with the single red star in a white disc on a green band – lay berthed at a Sun Shipbuilding jetty awaiting her final trials before hand-over to Texaco. Aboard, 100 or so men – crew, shipyard officials, Texaco representatives, technicians – pored over the gleaming new ship and her state-of-the-art machinery and equipment. On the bridge, her Texaco Master to be, Captain Sverre Petersen, for now contented himself with observing on the sidelines as the captain for the next couple of days, a shipyard man, watched hawsers fore and aft cast off.

---

* The deadweight of a merchant ship equates to the amount of cargo carried, plus bunker- and lubricating oils.

With her powerful turbines slow ahead, and a tug straining at a hawser attached to her forecastle, the big ship edged away from the jetty and out into the roadstead. Midstream the tug cast off and the big tanker felt the surge of the sea along her streamlined hull. "A little to the right", her captain instructed the helmsman (in the United States 'left' and 'right' replaced the more familiarly nautical 'port' and 'starboard'), as he scanned an expanse of water as familiar to him as the back of his hand. Down in the engine room, technicians and engineers from shipyard and new owners studied rpm, watched dials, pushed levers, checked water levels and lubricating oils, and listened to the throb and hum of these mighty machines intently, for the engines are the heart of any ship. By mid-afternoon the gleaming new tanker approached Overfalls, off the Delaware Capes, for adjustment of magnetic compasses, and calibration and final checks to her radio direction finder. Anchors were lowered and raised to test the relevant machinery and the ship anchored for the night off Delaware Breakwater, taking on ballast water in preparation for loaded speed trials the following day.

At 7.10am the following morning, the captain looked at his watch and moved the engine room telegraph to half-speed ahead. A slight quiver rippled through the ship as she got under way and a streak of white water curved past her prow. Now the captain moved the telegraph to full ahead and *Ohio,* ballasted to her loadline, surged forward, the streak of white water becoming a plume of white spray rolling ahead of her bow as she entered the measured mile for her speed trials 'with a bone in her teeth'. Eight runs were made and as if to save the best for last, on the final sprint she achieved a much better than expected 19¼ knots. Over the eight runs her average loaded speed at full power measured one and one quarter knots faster than her shipyard-guaranteed sixteen knots. More shakedowns followed ~ the time taken to make a full turn with rudder hard over; switching from full speed ahead to full speed astern, tests and more tests – and all passed with ease, to the delight of the shipyard and her new owners.

On completion of her trials and hand-over to Texaco, *Ohio* made her way to Port Arthur, Texas, to load her first commercial cargo, and in the ensuing weeks and months performed faultlessly. In July she underlined the high standard of her specification by completing a voyage from Bayonne, New Jersey, to Port Arthur, a distance of 1,882 miles, in four days twelve hours, at an average speed of over 17 knots.

23

That same 18 June 1940, as *Ohio* began her trials, German armies pressed relentlessly on with their invasion of France. Two days previously, Marshal Pétain had proposed an armistice, quickly agreed by Hitler on terms favourable to himself, and signed four days later. With the passing of a further forty-eight hours, Petain agreed and signed an armistice with Italy. The French fleet in the Mediterranean ceased to feature as an ally for the Royal Navy, and might even become an enemy. Malta was isolated.

# III

By the end of April 1942, the War Cabinet's assessment of Malta's vital food and fuel reserves was gloomy, (see CIGS memo page 14), and focused attention on re-supply. However, due to a shortage of ships, particularly escorts, the attempt would not be possible until June – perilously close to the final deadline. To make up for the deficiency, a decision was taken to run two convoys simultaneously, one from Alexandria in the Eastern Mediterranean, one via Gibraltar from the west. The operations, which would be completely autonomous, were designated *Vigorous* and *Harpoon* respectively. *Harpoon* comprised five freighters plus escort, and sailed from the Clyde on 4 June, passing through the Straits of Gibraltar on the night of the 11th/12th. Here the battleship *Malaya* strengthened the escort in company with the aircraft carrier *Eagle*. The large escorting force separated into squadrons, to each of which were assigned specific tasks. Force X, comprising the anti-aircraft cruiser *Cairo* and destroyers *Bedouin*, *Marne*, *Matchless*, *Ithuriel*, *Partridge*, *Blankney*, *Middleton*, *Badsworth* and *Kujawiak*, plus four minesweepers, would form the close escort to take the convoy through to Malta. Thanks to the efforts of Sir Ralph Metcalfe, heading the Tanker Division of the Ministry of War Transport in London, and Sir Arthur Salter, leading the British Merchant Shipping Mission to Washington, also joining the convoy at Gibraltar was the U.S. tanker *Kentucky*, owned by Texaco, and a sister vessel to the *Ohio*. Negotiations for the loan of *Kentucky* had been delicate, and succeeded in the face of opposition from, among others, H. Harris Robson, General Director of Shipping for the United States, who believed that all America's large fast tankers were needed for national defence. Carrying a full cargo of fuel oil and kerosene, her passage from Philadelphia to Gibraltar, where she embarked a largely British crew, was her maiden voyage.

To counter *Harpoon*, the Italian *Commando Supremo* disposed a force of submarines, torpedo boats, surface warships and aircraft to cover all routes to the islands.

Air attacks commenced on the morning of 14 June, and a running battle ensued for most of the day. A freighter was sunk, and by that evening, as the convoy passed to the north of Bizerta and turned to approach The Narrows, *Malaya* and the heavy ships turned back to Gibraltar as planned, leaving Force X to escort the remaining merchantmen to Malta.

At dawn on 15 June, with Pantelleria on the convoy's port beam, reconnaissance aircraft from Malta spotted an Italian formation of three cruisers and five destroyers approaching some fifteen miles away, and signalled Captain C. Hardy, Senior Officer of the escort in *Cairo*. Realising that his 8 x 4" (101mm) anti-aircraft guns had little prospect of holding off the Italian squadron, Hardy turned convoy and escort away towards the neutral waters of Tunisia to gain time for an air strike to be launched from Malta. Despite this manoeuvre, the Italian warships quickly overhauled the lumbering merchantmen and the cruisers *Raimundo Montecucolli* and *Eugenio Di Savoia** opened fire, straddling *Cairo*. Hardy despatched five of his destroyers against the Italian squadron, while the remaining four covered the convoy with a smokescreen. As they sped to the attack, *Bedouin* and *Partridge* were quickly hit and stopped by accurate Italian gunnery, however, fearing a torpedo attack, Italian Admiral Da Zara edged his cruisers away, while ordering two of his destroyers to attack the convoy. A complicated series of thrusts and counter thrusts now ensued, and to confuse the mêlée further, Ju88 fighter bombers from Sicily swept in to attack the merchantmen in a perfectly timed attack that caught their escorts fully engaged with the Italian cruisers. A freighter was hit almost immediately and set afire, while near-miss bomb blasts shook *Kentucky* severely. The tanker's main steam pipe ruptured, her engines stopped, and she drifted to a halt. Taken in tow by a minesweeper, with a second standing guard as anti-aircraft protection, these three were left astern as the convoy headed on to Malta.

Having for the moment driven off Da Zara, assisted by the arrival of Beaufighters from Malta overhead, Hardy returned to his charges

---

* 'Condottieri' class, main armament 8 x 6" (152mm) guns.

and detailed *Ithuriel* to assist with *Kentucky*. More air attacks from Sicily developed, including the fearsome Ju87 'Stuka' dive-bombers, and the freighter *Burdwan* was hit and stopped. Captain Hardy now found himself in the unenviable position of being caught between powerful air and sea forces, with two crippled merchantmen to defend as well as the two remaining freighters – so far mercifully undamaged. Reluctantly he ordered *Burdwan* and *Kentucky* sunk so as to concentrate on fighting the undamaged ships through to Malta. Having taken off the stricken merchantmen's crews, *Ithuriel* and the minesweepers attempted to despatch *Kentucky* but, demonstrating the strength of the type, she would not sink, and was eventually sent to the bottom by a torpedo from the Italian destroyer *Oriani*, as the British warships withdrew before the returning Italian cruiser squadron.

In the United States there was a certain amount of disquiet both within Texaco and the Roosevelt administration at what was seen as the 'abandonment' of *Kentucky*. It was suggested that the broken steam pipe might have been repaired and that the ship might have continued under her own power, but those making the suggestions were not on board under severe air and sea attack. There were mistakes in the planning of the operation however, as Force X was simply not strong enough for the tasks it was called upon to perform. Nevertheless the *Kentucky* episode had not been a total loss, as she had shown that these otherwise superb ships had an Achilles heel when under fire. Steps would be taken to ensure that their engines were not so easily disabled in the future.

★   ★   ★   ★

The Alexandria convoy fared no better than *Harpoon*. Setting out on 11 June with eleven merchantmen escorted by eight cruisers and twenty-six destroyers, the *Vigorous* enterprise was beset by conflicting orders arising from confusion over the precise location and intentions of a powerful Italian battle group, which included the battleships *Littorio* and *Vittorio Veneto*. This confusion led to the convoy being turned back to Alexandria, and about-face to Malta several times, losing merchantmen and escorts in the process to air, torpedo-boat, and submarine attack. Finally the convoy was recalled and re-entered Alexandria on 16 June, having lost six merchantmen, three destroyers and a cruiser. An officer aboard a British cruiser summed up the enterprise as *'an Imperial balls-up'*.[2]

Of the seventeen merchant ships despatched in the double convoy operations, the two freighters from *Harpoon*, finally escorted in to Grand Harbour by Captain Hardy, were the only ships to get through to Malta. The vital food stocks carried in these vessels might stave off surrender until September, but it would be a very close run thing, particularly without replenishment of dwindling reserves of kerosene for cooking.

★   ★   ★   ★

Winston Churchill and the War Cabinet now faced two incompatible problems. A convoy must be fought through to Malta, while on the Russian front the Red Army suffered horrendous losses in men and equipment, and Stalin's demands for a convoy to Murmansk became increasingly strident. There were simply not enough merchant ships or escorts to do both. In order to ensure that *Operation Harpoon* could be mounted to Malta, the June convoy to Russia had been cancelled. There was now no option but to encourage Malta to hold on while a convoy was organised and despatched to Murmansk. On 27 June 1942, the thirty-five merchant ships of convoy PQ17 departed the Icelandic port of Hvalfjord, and sailed to meet their tragic fate in the chill waters of the Barents Sea.

From the moment it became apparent that *Vigorous* and *Harpoon* would fail to get enough ships through to Malta, plans were laid for the next attempt, to be made as soon as ships, especially escorts, were available. This was estimated to be August, and once again desperately close to the deadline. For this convoy the cream of the British merchant marine would be required – fast cargo liners with a minimum speed requirement of 16 knots, plus, essentially, a large fast tanker, which, put simply, <u>must</u> get through for Malta to survive. Even with supplies of food and other essentials from the freighters, without kerosene for cooking, the islands would starve. A number of the island's generators were coal-fired, but without fuel for the oil burners, production of electricity for civilian and military use would fail, and Malta would slowly grind to a halt. There also remained the core reason for all the costly effort to date – the military imperative to rebuild the operational capability of the island. Rommel's supply convoys must be destroyed, and the most effective way to ensure that end was to return Malta to the attack. In order to regain maximum offensive capacity, significant quantities of oil for submarines and surface ships were required to replenish exhausted stocks. The British merchant marine, the largest fleet in the world by far, was again

27

scoured for a suitable ship, but a familiar problem reared its head. There were no large tankers fast enough to keep up with a 16-knot convoy.

On 17 June, Winston Churchill departed on the twenty-seven hour flight to Washington for discussions with President Franklin D. Roosevelt – latest in what was becoming a regular series of meetings between the two war leaders. Once again, exhaustive investigations had shown that the only tankers large enough and fast enough for the Malta operation were the Texaco ships. Investigations also revealed *Ohio* to have departed Sinclair Terminal, Houston, Texas, on 25 May with a full cargo of gasoline, bound for the U.K. Her ETA at Bowling, on the Clyde, was 21 June[3], making her the first U.S. tanker to arrive in Britain following Pearl Harbor and the full entry of the United States into the war. She not only fitted the bill perfectly, she was perfectly placed, and on 18 June General Ismay, Churchill's Chief of Staff, suggested to the Prime Minister that an approach might be made to Texaco via Roosevelt for her use in the upcoming Malta convoy. This would be a ticklish subject, as elements within Texaco and the U.S. administration were still unhappy at the recent loss of *Kentucky*. As related in connection with negotiations for the loan of that ship, powerful voices were raised within the American government urging that, with the United States fully engaged in the war, these large fast ships should be retained for the nation's own use. Releasing *Ohio* for the exact same mission as her ill-starred sister vessel would not be popular.

During talks at Roosevelt's Hyde Park house in New York State on 18 June, Prime Minister Churchill and the President further refined details for *Operation Torch*, the impending invasion of North Africa originally scheduled for the spring of 1942, but now planned for the latter part of the year. Malta was ideally placed on the eastern flank of the proposed landings in Algeria to seriously disrupt any air and sea attacks against the invasion forces, or attempts at Axis reinforcement of their land forces. This weighed in the balance in favour of preventing the surrender of the islands; however, matters of an infinitely more far-reaching nature were also on the agenda. Under detailed discussion was the development of an atomic bomb.

In Britain research into the A-bomb, code-named Tube Alloys, was at least as far advanced as research in the United States, possibly farther. For reasons of convenience, security, and speed (since Germany was also known to be at work on a nuclear device), Prime Minister Churchill agreed at this meeting that all Britain's research would be put at the disposal of the United States[4], and that, although Britain would remain an equal partner in the project, all future research would be carried out in the United States. The conclusion of such a momentous agreement must have considerably smoothed the path for an approach to the U.S. President, made quite possibly on the same day, on the subject of the loan of a tanker.

The United States Maritime Commission duly requisitioned *Ohio* from Texaco and delivered her on bareboat[5] charter to Britain's Ministry of War Transport, to be operated by the Eagle Oil and Shipping Company under British flag.

## Notes

[1]   The largest ships then afloat with electrically welded hulls were German pocket-battleships of the 'Lützow' (ex-'Deutschland') class, which had a length of 609'3" (185.7m).

[2]   *MALTA CONVOYS*, Richard Woodman, John Murray (Publishers) Ltd., 2000, p. 367.

[3]   Chevron Texaco Archives, California, USA.

[4]   *CHURCHILL*, Roy Jenkins, Macmillan, 2001, p. 691.

[5]   A form of charter in which the charterer becomes the 'disponent owner' (owner of the ship in all but name), crewing, insuring and operating the ship as the owner, in return for payment of a significantly lower charter rate to the actual owner.

# CHAPTER THREE

# PREPARATIONS

## I

The Eagle Oil and Shipping Company (initially the Eagle Oil Transport Co.), first saw the light of day in 1912, formed by Weetman Pearson, engineer, Member of Parliament, oil prospector, subsequently the first Viscount Cowdray, and, like Joseph Cullinan of Texaco, one of those larger than life entrepreneurs who come along from time to time to enliven the dusty balance sheets of corporate profit and loss. Samuel Pearson founded the family business, S. Pearson & Son, in Bradford, Yorkshire, in 1856. The business prospered, and when Samuel died in 1879, Weetman's father George took over. Weetman Pearson also joined the family enterprise and in 1894 became the sole partner at the age of thirty-eight. By this time the company had blossomed into a substantial engineering contractor at home and abroad, counting among works successfully completed the Mexico Drainage Canal, the Blackwall Tunnel under the Thames, the central section of the Lancashire, Derbyshire and East Coast Railway, the Avila and Salamanca Railway and the Hudson Tunnel. The capital of the company amounted to £500,000 in Preference shares and £1,000,000 in Ordinary shares, all owned by Weetman and family.[1]

Although preferring the cut and thrust of business life to the (then) more orderly proceedings of the House of Commons, Weetman Pearson agreed to stand as the Liberal candidate for Colchester, and was elected in 1895 at his second attempt. He was to hold the seat for fifteen years.

Not everything that Pearson touched turned to gold however, and, ironically, a major loss-making venture for the company involved Malta. In 1901, the Admiralty appointed S. Pearson & Co. to rebuild the existing docks and construct two new docks in Grand Harbour. Unexpected problems arose from massive ingress of water through fissures into the excavations (at times as much as 45,000,000 gallons *per day*), and required the installation of an exceptionally powerful (and expensive) pumping plant before work could continue. Completion was held up for two years, at the end of which the company found itself out of pocket to the tune of £265,000, which the Admiralty declined to reimburse.[2]

Weetman Pearson had a long association with Mexico, involving a number of large construction projects. Returning from a business trip in April 1901, the Yorkshireman missed a connection and had to 'stop over' at Laredo, Texas, for nine hours. Finding the place wild with excitement over recent discoveries of oil, he recalled a surveyors' report noting oil seepage on land granted as a subvention to the company in Pedregal, Mexico. Seizing the moment he cabled company headquarters, now in London, instructing them to '*secure option not only on oil land, but all land for miles around*'[3].

Burgeoning Mexican oil interests brought Pearson directly into conflict with the American Waters Pierce Oil Company, owned one-third by Henry Clay Pierce, two-thirds by the Standard Oil Company, and prior to the Yorkshireman's intervention in 1901, enjoying a virtual monopoly of oil sales in and from Mexico. Extensive and extended negotiations with Waters Pierce having failed to reach a compromise agreement, Pearson decided to take them on. In order to successfully fight off Waters Pierce and Standard Oil, he realised that it would be necessary to control all aspects of his oil business – production, refinement, distribution and sales. This entailed the formation of a company to own and operate oil tankers, and Eagle Oil Transport, later to become Eagle Oil and Shipping, came into being. The company's ships would be named for saints in the Mexican calendar and carry the prefix *San*. Important contracts were concluded with the British Admiralty and other major organisations, and so well-established did the Mexican venture become, that by 1912 Aguila, Pearson's production company, had contracted to provide erstwhile rivals Standard Oil with 10,000,000 barrels of crude oil.[4]

On the outbreak of the First World War in 1914, Pearson's Mexican wells were producing millions of barrels of oil per day, and a profitable speculation turned overnight into a vital British national resource.

Weetman Pearson died in 1927, but Eagle Oil continued to flourish, and with the coming of war again in 1939 owned twenty-nine tankers, all of which would endure the hazards of the times, some inevitably to be lost, and some, including *San Demetrio* which was owned, and *Ohio*, taken on charter, to write indelible feats of courage and endurance into the pages of maritime history.

## II

*Ohio* made her providential Atlantic voyage alone, without convoy or escort,[5] arriving at Bowling on the appointed day, 21 June. Having discharged her cargo, steam-cleaned and gas-freed her tanks, she shifted out to the roadstead to anchor and await orders. Her Master, Captain Sverre Petersen (see Appendix 2 for crew list), found himself the recipient of a letter from Lord Leathers, Britain's Minister of War Transport, offering a personal welcome *'at your safe arrival in the Clyde with the first cargo of oil carried in a United States tanker'*[6], but of the discussions concerning the tanker's fate there was no hint.

That fate had in fact been settled on 22 June, the day following her arrival, when Thomas Buchanan, General Manager of the Texas Company Marine Department in New York, telegraphed Mr A.J. Singleton, the Texaco agent in London, notifying him that the U.S.M.C. *'have requisitioned title to unit your 660 [Ohio] . . . understand . . . in turn will assign on bareboat MOWT with transfer to British flag . . . In view specialized design consider advisable portion our crew particularly engineers stand by for purpose familiarization new crew'*[7].

One or two procedural details remained to be smoothed over for the ship's transfer to British flag, and there were further discussions as to the suitability and advisability of using this vessel for what was guaranteed to be an exceptionally hazardous voyage, but there was never any real doubt that *Ohio* would be going to Malta. Alternatives were conspicuous only by their absence. So it was that on the 23rd a launch took Singleton and a representative of the Ministry of War Transport out to the big new tanker as she swung easily at her moorings. 'Snowy' Petersen (from his shock of white hair) welcomed the two men into his cabin, but the welcome quickly cooled as Singleton explained that he and his crew were to lose the ship which, for many of them, had been their home since her first voyage in 1940. Singleton had little more than the sketchy details given him in the cable from Buchanan, but *did* now know that *Ohio* was earmarked for a strictly hush-hush convoy. The man from the Ministry undoubtedly knew more, but was forbidden to say. Why, Captain Petersen not unnaturally wanted to know, could he and his crew not take the ship on the convoy, but it was explained that she would transfer to British flag, and therefore take aboard a British crew, and that was that.

The crew were told to pack their gear as, with the exception of a number of engineers, they would be leaving the ship to await passage home. Second Engineer James Murphy would remain to assist the incoming British crew, but noted that *'there was quite a scramble, considering the amount of gear a person can collect in two years on board ship. Not having enough bags, the Chief Mate turned the deck department to making canvas seabags'*[8].

For the American crew a final task remained: to assist tugs in moving *Ohio* to Stobross Quay, where on 25 June she was handed over to a representative of the United States Maritime Commission[9]. There was no ceremony for the transfer to a British flag: one morning the Stars and Stripes were hauled down from her jack staff, and the Red Duster raised. On 30 June, the Glasgow pilot came aboard, and at 14.10hrs a scratch crew and the busy little tugs shifted her to Princes Dock, where she arrived at 15.50 the same day[10].

For her passage from the United States, *Ohio*'s smart Texaco colour scheme disappeared under a coat of wartime 'battleship' grey, and she carried a 5" (127mm) gun, and a 3" (76.2mm) anti-aircraft gun. At Princes Dock her armament would be substantially strengthened, and a number of additional modifications carried out to prepare the ship for what lay ahead across 3,000 miles of ocean.

★ ★ ★ ★

By the time work commenced in Princes Dock, the additional merchant ships that would make up *Operation Pedestal*, the codename for this last-ditch attempt to re-supply Malta, had been earmarked. These were all fine ships, which, during the course of July, were drawn together from ports around the United Kingdom to assemble at Gourock, also on the Clyde. They were the British flag *Wairangi* (12,313 tons deadweight, built 1935, 17 knots), *Waimarama* (13,000 tons deadweight, built 1938, 16.5 knots), *Empire Hope* (12,688 tons gross*, built 1941, 16 knots), *Glenorchy* (9,500 tons deadweight, built 1939, 18 knots), *Melbourne Star* (11,800 tons deadweight, built 1936, 16 knots), *Brisbane Star* (11,519 tons deadweight, built 1936, 16 knots), *Dorset* (13,650 tons deadweight, built 1934, 16 knots),

* Gross tonnage equates to approximately the total enclosed space of the ship, calculated at 100 cubic feet per ton.

33

*Deucalion* (8,930 tons deadweight, built 1930, 16 knots), *Rochester Castle* (9,256 tons deadweight, built 1937, 16.5 knots), *Clan Ferguson* (10,160 tons deadweight, built 1938, 16 knots), and from the United States the *Santa Elisa* (9,020 tons deadweight, built 1940, 16 knots) and the brand-new *Almeria Lykes* (12,830 tons deadweight, built 1942, 16 knots). As each ship arrived, she would be sent alongside to have existing anti-aircraft armament augmented by the addition of extra Bofors, Oerlikon and Browning machine guns (see Appendix 3 for additional details).

All thirteen of these fast cargo liners would load a similarly mixed cargo – aviation spirit and kerosene in 4 gallon cans (in some cases trucks filled with more cans, and loaded tanker wagons were to be lashed on deck), all manner of ammunition, bombs, torpedoes, etc., foodstuffs and flour, bagged coal, plus small quantities of 'luxury' items – chocolate, cigarettes, wine, etc. Mail would be carried in cargo lockers and strong rooms. The cargoes were split between ships so that if even one got through, Malta would receive at least a little of each of the essential supplies required. The exception of course was *Ohio*, as only she could carry the oil so urgently needed in sufficient quantities to enable Malta to fight on.

To escort these fourteen merchant vessels, the Royal Navy assembled the most powerful fleet of warships that it was to muster for a single operation during the entire war (see Appendix 4), comprising, from the U.K. to Cape Bon, two battleships, four aircraft carriers, seven light cruisers, thirty-four destroyers, three Royal Naval Auxiliary tankers for refuelling at sea, seven corvettes and an ocean-going tug. In view of Axis air strength in Sicily, at Cape Bon a large portion of the fleet would return to Gibraltar, leaving for the escort through the Narrows to Malta, four light cruisers and eleven destroyers. Assisting as soon as *Pedestal* got within range would be Malta's Spitfires and Beaufighters, vectored in by RAF fighter direction officers with ship to air communications equipment aboard two of the cruisers. The Tenth Submarine Flotilla, having recently returned to Malta (and desperate for fuel from *Ohio*), would deploy its seven submarines to screen the convoy from any Italian warships threatening an attack.

The armada gathering for 'Pedestal' included the Type II 'Hunt' class escort destroyer *Ledbury*, captained by the rumbustuous Roger Hill, described by a fellow captain as being a natural rebel, with tons of zip, pep and go, who would in earlier times have made an excellent pirate, albeit a very humane one. Warships for the Malta convoy were drawn together from as far afield as the Indian Ocean, and *Ledbury* herself initially formed part of the screen covering a troop convoy outward bound from the U.K. to Egypt via the Cape of Good Hope, with reinforcements for the Eighth Army in the Western Desert. She was, however, ordered to break off at Gibraltar and join Force X, that part of the *Pedestal* defence designated to take the merchantmen through to Malta (see Appendix 4).

Prior to escorting the troopships, *Ledbury* took part in the disastrous PQ17 convoy to Murmansk during which the Admiralty, fearing an attack by a powerful battle group led by the battleship *Tirpitz*, ordered the merchantmen to scatter to give them a better chance of survival against surface attack. The escort, including *Ledbury*, received unequivocal orders to withdraw. While scattering may have made freighters and tankers less likely to be tracked and sunk by surface ships, it also laid them open to serious hazard from other predators and as a result aircraft and U-boat attacks picked them off with ease, to the extent that the *Tirpitz* battle group found itself recalled without getting into action, there being no further need for an offensive by surface ships. Of the thirty-four merchantmen with the convoy twenty-three were sunk. As *Ledbury* withdrew, she picked up a series of signals from the ships of the convoy on the Merchant Navy wavelength – *'Am being bombed by large number of planes . . .', 'Abandoning ship . . .', 'Six U-Boats approaching on the surface . . .', 'On fire in the ice'*. Trapped between fire and ice, 153 merchant seamen died. Hill considered turning back, but, *'discipline is strong, our orders were clear, we were miles away by then, and . . . almost out of fuel'*[11].

For the crew of *Ledbury* the shame of being ordered to leave their colleagues in the Merchant Navy cut deeply, and Roger Hill determined that, regardless of orders, in future no merchantman would be left to its fate while he and his ship were capable of doing anything about it.

★   ★   ★   ★

As the convoy took shape, work continued on *Ohio* including the fitting of Oerlikon anti-aircraft guns on platforms at either side of the midships Boat Deck, a Bofors gun and platform to the Poop Deck, aft end centre, and minesweeping paravanes to the forecastle deck.

Additional anti-aircraft armament in the form of P.A.C. (Parachute and Cable) rocket launchers were fitted to a platform on top of the midships superstructure (monkey island), above the wheelhouse. Each rocket would carry a cable attached to a parachute and Mills bomb 500 feet (152.4m) into the air, the object being to snag the wings of attacking aircraft and bring them down. Despite sounding something of a Heath-Robinson affair, it achieved a measure of success, and is credited with going some way towards discouraging bombing runs at masthead height by Axis aircraft[12]. There were two main disadvantages with this ingenious weapon, the first being that as the lanyard for firing the rockets was placed in the wheelhouse, there existed the possibility of its mistaken use instead of the siren lanyard, and second the nagging suspicion that, given the appropriate wind strength and direction, parachute and bomb might drop gently back onto the ship, with potentially disastrous results.

The tally of *Ohio*'s armament advanced to six Oerlikon, one Bofors, and two Browning machine guns, plus the 3" (76.2mm) high angle gun forward, the 5" (127mm) low angle gun aft, four sets of P.A.C. rockets, and the minesweeping paravanes[13]. This was a substantial amount of weaponry for a merchant ship, even in these hazardous times, and in order to accommodate the extra gunners and naval personnel (crew for this trip would number seventy-seven), many of the single berth cabins were adapted to twin-berth. The *Kentucky* experience was very much in mind as the refit progressed, and on the advice of Royal Naval Engineer Lieutenant Commander Woolnough, modifications were made to the main engines to make them less susceptible to damage from the shock of near-miss bomb blast, including the replacement of any cast iron piping with less brittle steel fittings.

One further indispensable equipment system remained to be installed. As a result of wartime experience, Mr Lynn Nelson, chief of the Eagle Oil technical staff, had in 1940 developed a compressed air system to aid the salvage of torpedoed ships at sea (see diagram page 37). Tankers of this period would normally be equipped with two air-compressors in the engine room, to which, for the Nelson system, a third would be added in a forward compartment. The three compressors were connected by an air line running the entire length of the ship along which, at points adjacent to the tank lids, quick-action connections would be fitted, enabling the instantaneous connection of air hoses. In the event that the hull were to be holed, an air hose would be connected to the tank or tanks affected, the tank lids screwed down tight, and compressed air pumped into the damaged compartments. Rising water would first be halted then expelled as pressure increased, until the tank became buoyant with compressed air[14].

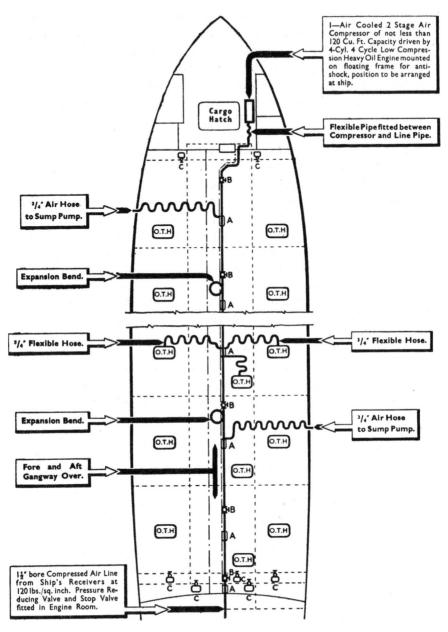

The following labels appear on the diagram:

**I—Air Cooled 2 Stage Air Compressor** of not less than 120 Cu. Ft. Capacity driven by 4-Cyl. 4 Cycle Low Compression Heavy Oil Engine mounted on floating frame for anti-shock, position to be arranged at ship.

**Flexible Pipe fitted between Compressor and Line Pipe.**

Cargo Hatch

**³/₄" Air Hose to Sump Pump.**

**Expansion Bend.**

**³/₄" Flexible Hose.**

**³/₄" Flexible Hose.**

**Expansion Bend.**

**³/₄" Air Hose to Sump Pump.**

**Fore and Aft Gangway Over.**

**1½" bore Compressed Air Line** from Ship's Receivers at 120 lbs./sq. inch. Pressure Reducing Valve and Stop Valve fitted in Engine Room.

O.T.H

*Diagram courtesy of the Shell Oil Co.*

The Eagle Oil compressed-air salvage system, which became standard equipment on board all tankers.

The system was extremely versatile, being capable of pumping seawater for firefighting should the engine-room pumps be damaged, and for the transference of cargo from a damaged tank isolated by ruptured cargo lines and therefore incapable of discharge in the normal way. To achieve this, a submersible air-pump would be lowered into the tank and compressed air utilised to force the cargo through a flexible pipe leading from the tank lid of the damaged compartment to a secure tank. The air-lines could also be coupled to the steering gear and used to steer the ship by compressed air, should the usual power sources fail[15].

The third compressor for *Ohio*, Model 125 made by the Consolidated Pneumatic Tool Co., Fraserburgh, was removed from hull 1163 building at the Harland and Wolff Shipyard, Govan, fitted under the forecastle head of the tanker, and connected to an existing air-line, which then had the necessary modifications made to allow the fitment of air hoses to individual tanks.

The compressed air system was one of a number of wartime innovations developed by Eagle Oil technicians, another being the Eagle Protective Mask, designed to prevent the real possibility of suffocation risked by tanker crews abandoning their stricken ships into waters fouled by hundreds of tons of oil. The mask comprised a thin rubber hood designed to fit closely over the head, with a valve positioned high over the forehead. The valve was kept closed as the crewman jumped into the oil-covered sea, then opened as he surfaced by a tap of the hand on a disc attachment. The great advantage of the valve developed and used with the mask was that neither oil nor water could penetrate, but air was easily breathed. A further innovation concerned the eye-pieces, which comprised three thin transparent discs in front of plain glass, held in place by adhesive rings with tabs attached, enabling the removal of one disc at a time by tugging a tab with the fingers. For a man immersed in an oily sea the benefits were immense, allowing him to maintain some sort of vision while getting his bearings. Swimming blindly away from wreckage, rafts, or lifeboats that might have saved him, cost many a tanker crewman his life[16].

# III

Ray Morton took a moment from his duties to contemplate the ship on which he sailed as she trudged homeward across the Bay of Biscay with a cargo of iron ore. The eleven-year-old bulk carrier *Camerata* was, he concluded, a *'battered old rust bucket'*. In the grey damp winter of 1940/41 Ray left home in County Durham for the sea, and having spent six months as a deck boy and twelve months as a cabin boy, now looked forward to his next berth, and possible promotion to Assistant Steward. This was June 1942, and he had just turned eighteen years old.

*Camerata* berthed on Tyneside, but shipping was quiet in the north-east and the Merchant Navy Pool in Newcastle sent Ray to Glasgow to join a big new tanker called the *Ohio,* (or 'O' 'H' 'ten' as the crew nicknamed her). Despite the fact that her destination was still strictly classified, with memories of the well-used bulk carrier still fresh in his mind, Ray could barely believe his luck as he walked up the gangway and signed on:

*She was a luxury compared with the ships I had sailed in. Two-berth cabins and food we had only dreamed about. She had been provisioned in the U.S.A. and had grapefruit in the cool rooms, a dozen varieties of cereal for breakfast, followed by bacon and eggs! A whole variety of meat and fish and ice-cream!*[17]

Sixty years after the event his enthusiasm is still palpable! At the time, elation with his new berth was fuelled by confirmation of his promotion to Assistant Steward, and a salary increment to £14.00 per month, to include a £4.00 War Risk or 'danger money' supplement.

The young Ray Morton was as full of vinegar and youthful exuberance as any teenager, but had been raised a member of a God-fearing family – and this was war. Consequently, when he went off to sea he took a pocket-sized copy of the Bible, presented to him in 1939 for good attendance at Sunday school. On the flyleaf a label had been attached denoting the name of the Parish, his name and the reason for the presentation, the year, signature of the vicar, and in small print at the bottom the name of a Bible and Tract Society together with their address. Ray carefully placed the Bible in his cabin aboard ship.

The new crew for *Ohio* assembled from the length and breadth of the British Isles – from the Isle of Barra in the north to Chalfont St Giles in the south, South Shields in the east to County Meath in the west. Numbered among the new arrivals, and still mystified by his urgent instructions to report to the tanker, forty-year-old Chief Engineer James Wyld came aboard accompanied by Eagle's Glasgow agent, W. Nelson. Wyld was a senior engineer for the Eagle Company currently engaged in overseeing machinery installation into their new building tanker *San Veronico* at Harland & Wolff's Belfast shipyard. What, he wondered, could be so pressing that it demanded he be dragged away from this highly specialised and important work? Wyld hailed from Glasgow, and was a fine example of the tradition that Scotland has for producing outstanding engineers. He was also a long-time Eagle employee, having joined in 1918 as a Junior Engineer. The company was quick to recognise his talents, and appointments followed to Third Engineer in 1920, Second Engineer in 1922, and Chief Engineer in 1937. Whilst in this last capacity, aboard *San Felix*, he earned a commendation for services in action.

Wyld attempted to discover from the agent what all the fuss was about, but Nelson cannily suggested he first take a look around the engine room. With that mixture of awe and itchy fingers that engineers have when confronted by big, new, state-of-the-art power plants, James Wyld took time to acclimatise himself to pipes, boilers, turbines, gauges and the innovative electronic controls required to keep these magnificent beasts operating smoothly. By the time he returned to the agent it is safe to assume that he was fairly salivating at the prospect of getting his hands on those engines, so when Nelson asked if he would like to sign on as Chief for an important trip, he jumped at the chance. Wyld then buttonholed Second Engineer James Murphy from the U.S. crew and disappeared back into the engine room to get to know his new charges in greater detail. Wyld was later to commend the level of assistance that he and other members of the incoming British crew received from the American engineers, particularly James Murphy.

For two more eighteen-year-olds, Ordinary Seamen Allan Shaw and his mate Ken Arundel, the situation at Goole, Yorkshire, was similar to that which greeted Ray Morton in Newcastle – 'nothing doing here, but there is a big new tanker in the Clyde . . .'

> *We went aboard the* Ohio *and got quite a pleasant surprise. A two year old American tanker, two men to a cabin, and a mess room fitted out with coffee machines on the boil twenty-four hours a day. It all seemed too good to be true . . .*[18]

Allan Shaw did have one gripe about the new ship, and that was 'The Bloody Monster' – a large emergency generator just installed in an alleyway in the crew's quarters aft (for ease of connection to the engine room below), just at the base of a companionway leading to the upper deck. During 'action stations' exercises, many a crewman barked his shins on the generator (no doubt to an accompaniment of suitably salty language), in his hurry to get up the companionway.

★ ★ ★ ★

It had originally been the intention of Eagle Oil to entrust *Ohio* to Captain Conrad Vidot, one of their more experienced skippers; however at the last moment the decision was amended in favour of Dudley Mason.

Dudley William Mason was born in Surbiton, Surrey, on 7 October 1901, both parents being in service with a family at nearby Long Ditton, where he and brother Charles also attended school. The boys were possessed of strong wills and great determination, and attended night school (at a time when such things were not always practical or easily arranged), with a resolute intention to better themselves. Charles subsequently qualified as a solicitor, having his own practice in Surbiton for many years, while Dudley moved, with his parents, to Westward Ho! on the North Devon coast. Dudley decided on a career at sea, and joined Eagle Oil as an apprentice officer on 1 September 1919.[19]

Eagle Oil and Dudley Mason took to each other from the start. The new apprentice liked the fact that the company operated as a 'family', everybody appearing to know everybody, from all serving at sea to the office staff at 16 Finsbury Circus, in the City of London.[20] Mason served his apprenticeship for four years, receiving an appointment to Third Mate in October 1924. Displaying characteristic purpose and determination, he had by that time already obtained his Second Mate's certificate, but sea time had to be put in before the higher rank could be confirmed, which it was in May 1927. Two months later the industrious twenty-six-year-old obtained his First Mate's certificate, and in February 1931, his Master's ticket. Eagle Oil appointed Dudley Mason temporary Master in August 1941, and confirmed his promotion to Master in 1942, just prior to sending him to the Clyde to join *Ohio*. At thirty-nine, Mason was the youngest Master in the Eagle fleet, and the company recognised that his performance had been outstanding. In selecting him to captain *Ohio* for the difficult and dangerous voyage to Malta, Eagle Oil acknowledged that '*Captain Mason was specially selected for this job, despite the fact that he is our most junior Master, on account of his proven initiative and efficiency, and splendid fortitude*'[21].

Captain Mason's exceptional seamanship was established and about to be put to its most severe test, but for stepdaughter Patricia her memories are of a wonderful father, possessed of a dry sense of humour *'which used to have us all in fits of laughter'*. His support for her and her own family in later years is still remembered with much affection. When ashore, the hard-working, energetic captain liked nothing better than to relax and unwind, and combined a keen interest in gardening with a fondness for cribbage and cricket[22].

On boarding his new command, Dudley Mason sought out James Wyld. The two were long time 'Eagle' men and good friends, having served together aboard *San Arcadio* when Mason had been Second Mate and Wyld Third Engineer. When Eagle Oil gave Mason the command they also gave him the pick of the company's officers to crew the ship, and his first choice for Chief Engineer had been 'Jimmy' Wyld. The two spent a lot of their spare time playing crib aboard *Arcadio*, and looked forward to another hand or two during the voyage to come. Another astute Mason choice, this time for Chief Officer, was Douglas Gray, a twenty-six-year-old Scot from Edinburgh, destined to prove himself not only on the voyage to come, but when subsequently given his first command.

In addition to a clutch of signallers and decoding operators, each merchant ship in *Pedestal* was assigned a Royal Naval liaison officer to assist communications between escort and convoy and to try to ensure a minimum of misunderstandings arising from the different methods employed by the two branches of the naval service. Posted to *Ohio* was Lieutenant Denys Barton, who (along with all the RN personnel and Army gunners), in order to comply with Board of Trade rules, found himself obliged to sign on as a deckhand at a wage of one shilling (5p) per month! Mason welcomed him aboard and enquired if he knew where they were bound, but having just returned from a stint with an anti-aircraft cruiser in the Eastern Mediterranean, the Lieutenant had heard nothing.

# IV

Keeping secret a combined fleet of merchant and naval vessels numbering over seventy was always going to present problems, but it was vital that the destination be kept under wraps for as long as possible. In an effort to disguise this key piece of intelligence the convoy was given the generic designation WS21S, 'WS' usually denoting a convoy outward bound from the U.K. to Suez via the Cape of Good Hope (affectionately known as 'Winston Specials').

With necessarily many thousands of crewmen and others involved with the convoy, 'scuttlebutt' was bound to be rife, and in at least one case latched on to the issuance of Mediterranean charts to naval vessels, and drew the inference that the destination must be Malta. There were also instances reported of cargo clearly marked 'Malta' being loaded aboard the merchantmen, to the extent that Admiral of the Fleet Lord Cork and Orrery broached the matter in Parliament during September 1942, and again in a debate in the House of Lords the following month.

## Notes

1  *WEETMAN PEARSON, THE FIRST VISCOUNT COWDRAY*, J.A. Spender, Cassell & Co., 1930, p. 26.
2  *Ibid.* p. 143/144.
3  *Ibid.* p. 149.
4  *Ibid.* pp. 170/171.
5  J.T. Murphy, Second Engineer, letter dated 29 October 1958, ChevronTexaco Archives, California, USA.
6  ChevronTexaco Archives, California, USA.
7  *Ibid.*
8  *Op.cit.* (Note 5).
9  *Op.cit.* (Note 6).
10 *SC88/5*, File 1, Shell Archive, Shell Centre, London. Shell handled certain aspects of ship management for Eagle Oil during the war years, and took the company over completely in the late 1950s.
11 *DESTROYER CAPTAIN*, Roger Hill, William Kimber & Co., 1975, p. 48.
12 *THE FOURTH SERVICE*, Merchantmen at War 1939-45, John Slader, New Era Writer's Guild (UK) Ltd., 1995, p. 60.
13 Report of Chief Officer D.G. Gray, *SC88*/File 1, Shell Archive, Shell Centre, London. See note 17 below.
14 *TANKER FLEET*, The War Story of the Shell Tankers and the Men who manned them, Stanton Hope, The Anglo-Saxon Petroleum Company, 1948, pp. 25/26.
15 *Ibid.*
16 *Ibid.* p. 95.
17 Ray Morton, in correspondence with the author. Regarding Note 13

above, Ray Morton's Action Station aboard *Ohio* was at a light machine gun on the port side of the aft boat deck. He is certain that the gun was a Hotchkiss, not a Browning. I can find no mention elsewhere of a Hotchkiss on board, but that does not mean there wasn't one, and since Ray Morton was there and I wasn't I am inclined to take his word for it –author.

[18] Allan Shaw, in correspondence with the author.

[19] Mrs Patricia Davis, Captain Mason's stepdaughter, in correspondence with the author.

[20] *Ibid.*

[21] Eagle Oil memorandum dated 19 August 1942, *SC88/5*, File 1, Shell Centre, London.

[22] *Op.cit.* Note 19.

# CHAPTER FOUR

# DEPARTURE

## I

By 24 July, most modifications to *Ohio* were completed and she shifted from Princes Dock back to Stobross Quay, bumping heavily against the Dock Knuckle Fendoff as she did so, damaging starboard side shell plating in way of No.11 cargo tank. Finishing touches were made to installation of the diesel generator plus works to lifeboats and life rafts, and on the following day she was scheduled to move to an oil wharf to commence loading cargo. However, due to a strike by tug personnel the move was cancelled. To avoid any longer delay than was absolutely necessary, the following two days saw several trips by barge back and forth to *Ohio* carrying diesel oil, which was duly pumped into Nos. 6 and 7 cargo tanks. The strike having been settled, on 27 July the big tanker moved to Bowling Oil Wharf to load kerosene, and from there to Loch Long to tie up alongside the tanker *Fjordaas*. From this former Norwegian vessel she loaded fuel oil into her remaining cargo tanks, plus bunker fuel for the voyage. Her final intake amounted to:

| | |
|---|---|
| *Diesel Oil* | *1,705.6 tons (1,733 tonnes)* |
| *Kerosene* | *1,894 tons (1,924 tonnes)* |
| *Fuel Oil* | *8,695 tons (8,834 tonnes)* |
| *Bunker fuel* | *1,300 tons (1,321 tonnes)* |
| *Lubricating oils* | *15 tons[1] (15.24 tonnes)* |

By the evening of the 30th loading had been completed and she shifted to anchorage in Loch Long to await orders. On 1 August, Direction Finder calibrations were made, and the ship was as ready as she ever would be for what lay ahead.

Command of Force X fell to Rear Admiral Harold M. Burrough, who would fly his flag in the 'Fiji' class light cruiser *Nigeria*. Burrough would oversee the convoy from the word go so that by the time they reached the Sicilian Narrows merchantmen and warships would be thoroughly moulded into a team, well used to working together. To assist this process, in addition to being able to contact each other and the convoy Commodore by radiotelephone, for the first time each merchant ship embarked a three-man naval signalling team.

A conference for all the merchant marine captains, led by Commodore A.G. Venables, was held in *Nigeria*'s aircraft hangar on 2 August. Venables would embark in *Port Chalmers*, and was one of a long list of former Royal Navy officers to come out of retirement during the Second World War in what turned out to be a highly successful system for placing officers with naval experience in senior positions with the merchantmen of a convoy. At the conference Burrough at last revealed that their destination was Malta, and, assisted by Venables, went over the whole operation in great detail, utilising models and diagrams. Burrough also, while perhaps trying not to display any trace of that irritation (tinged with envy) with which the 'free spirits' of the merchant marine were treated by the Senior Service, lay great emphasis on the need for strict discipline. On this trip a 'loose cannon' could signal disaster. The Admiral wound up by remarking that 12 August should see the convoy arriving at the Skerki Bank off Cape Bon, adding, '*You know what the 12th is. That's the day grouse shooting starts, and we should have plenty of birds in the Mediterranean*'[2].

Dudley Mason attended the conference accompanied by Lieutenant Barton, and on returning to *Ohio* found himself waylaid by several officers keen to know their destination. In practically no time 'Malta' was round the ship, and with the additional news that the convoy would sail that evening, she became a hive of activity.

August 2 had been, in that droll way that we have with regard to our weather, what the British like to refer to as a typical summer day – dull and overcast. Clyde River pilots were ordered for 18.30 hrs, at 20.00hrs windlasses stuttered into motion, anchor chains clanked, and the fourteen merchantmen on which the fate of Malta depended slowly got under way and, accompanied by *Nigeria* and several destroyers (for security reasons the bulk of the escort would join out to sea), formed up in pre-determined order. The first vessel, *Deucalion*, passed the North Channel boom outward bound at 20.30hrs, *Ohio* at 21.02hrs, and the last, *Almeria Lykes*, at 21.22hrs. Pilots were dropped and cutters carried them back to the river, while the ships of the convoy made their way out into the grey-green Atlantic swell and assembled in the four-column formation (see diagram page 48) which would be maintained for the greater part of the voyage. Notable exceptions would be passage of the Gibraltar Straits and the Sicilian Narrows, for which a two-column formation would be necessary.

As dawn broke on the morning of the 3rd, the crews of the merchantmen could scarcely believe their eyes, for the full extent of the escort was now revealed, with battleships, aircraft carriers, cruisers and destroyers as far as the eye could see, signal flags a-flutter, Aldis lamps blinking, and the whole mighty array steaming southwards on a broad front ten miles wide. *Ohio* held station astern of *Empire Hope* on the inner of the two starboard columns, and Ray Morton probably articulates the feelings of many of the merchant seamen that morning when he says that *'those bloody great sixteen inch gun battleships'*, and all the other escorts, *'made me feel ten feet tall!'*[3] There were two Assistant Stewards in addition to Ray: John Church and Raymond Banner, and all three busied themselves serving breakfast, tidying the officers' accommodation, and generally attending to duties assigned them by Chief Steward Francis Meeks and Second Steward John Stephens. Captain Mason had ordered the crew mustered aft in the Petty Officers' mess at 08.45hrs, and there was an expectant buzz about the ship that morning.

To the assembled company Mason explained the momentous nature of their mission, gave additional detail concerning their escort, and read a letter of encouragement from the management of Eagle Oil. A further letter, from A.V. Alexander, First Lord of the Admiralty, said in part:

*Before you start on this operation the First Sea Lord and I are anxious that you should know how grateful the Board of The Admiralty are to you for undertaking this difficult task. Malta has for some time been in great danger. It is imperative that she should be kept supplied. These are her critical months, and we cannot fail her. She has stood up to the most violent attack from the air that has ever been made, and now she needs your help in continuing the battle.*
*Her courage is worthy of yours.*[4]

47

# Convoy dispositions – 2 August [5]

## (including Masters and designated numbers)

*Distance between columns six cables – approximately 2,027 yards (1,853 metres).*

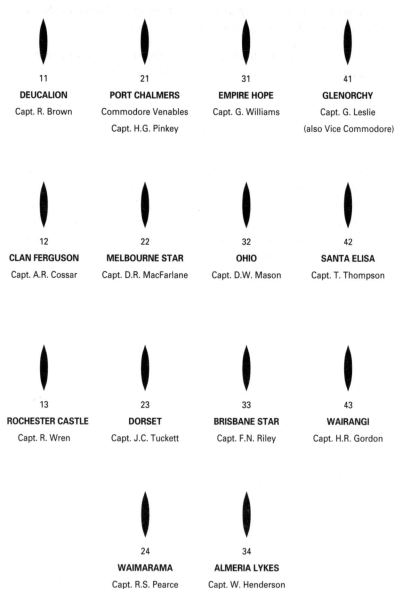

| 11 | 21 | 31 | 41 |
|---|---|---|---|
| **DEUCALION** | **PORT CHALMERS** | **EMPIRE HOPE** | **GLENORCHY** |
| Capt. R. Brown | Commodore Venables | Capt. G. Williams | Capt. G. Leslie |
| | Capt. H.G. Pinkey | | (also Vice Commodore) |

| 12 | 22 | 32 | 42 |
|---|---|---|---|
| **CLAN FERGUSON** | **MELBOURNE STAR** | **OHIO** | **SANTA ELISA** |
| Capt. A.R. Cossar | Capt. D.R. MacFarlane | Capt. D.W. Mason | Capt. T. Thompson |

| 13 | 23 | 33 | 43 |
|---|---|---|---|
| **ROCHESTER CASTLE** | **DORSET** | **BRISBANE STAR** | **WAIRANGI** |
| Capt. R. Wren | Capt. J.C. Tuckett | Capt. F.N. Riley | Capt. H.R. Gordon |

| 24 | 34 |
|---|---|
| **WAIMARAMA** | **ALMERIA LYKES** |
| Capt. R.S. Pearce | Capt. W. Henderson |

Mason finished with a few words of his own:

*You men have been specially chosen for this voyage, you probably wouldn't choose it yourself, but just remember that you are chosen men. I want no dodgers, no questions asked when an order is given . . . I don't expect it's going to be a picnic but . . . I've no doubt whatever that you will keep up the traditions of the Merchant Service, if the occasion demands. I have the utmost faith in you all.*[6]

Loud and spontaneous cheering greeted the speech, followed by jokes and much ersatz grumbling as the men dispersed to their duties.

# II

Overall command of Force F, the vast *Pedestal* armada which included Burrough's Force X, rested with Vice Admiral Sir E. Neville Syfret in the battleship *Nelson*. For the voyage down to Gibraltar Syfret planned a relentless series of manoeuvres and exercises designed to drum into merchantmen and escorts alike what was required of them when the inevitable attacks occurred. Emergency changes in course and speed, all to be carried out in formation, were to be second nature. Things might have been worse, as Allan Shaw recalls:

*Practising zigzag courses all the way down to Gibraltar was pretty easy. Ships doing sixteen knots are easier to handle and quicker to manoeuvre; that's a big difference to a slow convoy doing seven/eight knots.*[7]

The convoy had already experienced its first drama when, just prior to its departure from the Clyde, the destroyer *Lamerton*, en route to join the escort, was in collision with the freighter *Almenara* in thick fog. *Lamerton* suffered serious bow damage and was forced to return to the U.K., to be replaced at short notice as *Pedestal* sailed, by the destroyer *Keppel*, a veteran of PQ17.

★　★　★　★

That other veteran of the fateful Russia convoy, *Ledbury*, departed Northern Ireland on 30 July to join the escort of the troop-carrying convoy which she was to accompany as far as Gibraltar. Out in the Atlantic some way ahead of *Pedestal*, she was about to experience a drama of her own as a result of bad weather. Troopships and escort encountered thick patches of fog and Roger Hill noticed on the destroyer's radar screen that the port columns of merchantmen had strayed a mile or two from the convoy. For all the world like a fretting sheepdog, *Ledbury* raced after them and gently shepherded them back into position. As this was in progress, the starboard portion of the convoy remained shrouded in fog, while overhead and to port the weather cleared.

By this time *Ledbury* also had an aircraft on her radar, soon visually identified as a Sunderland from Coastal Command on anti-submarine patrol. As Hill and his officers watched, the big flying boat turned and droned in low over the convoy from the starboard side. *'Bloody fool'*, someone remarked, *'those ships will think he's attacking them'*. No sooner were the words spoken than nervous trigger fingers aboard several of the merchantmen twitched, and streams of ack ack fire arced towards the aircraft. Losing height, its starboard engine well afire, the Sunderland flew low over *Ledbury* as the destroyer worked up to full speed and followed the aircraft out. The speeding warship passed through patchy fog and Hill watched the Sunderland ditch and settle on the water, the crew scrambling onto a wing and waving at the rapidly approaching warship. While still some way off, Hill ordered *Ledbury* to slow and prepared to go alongside the wallowing flying boat and pick up the crew. As *Ledbury* edged closer, the aircraft sank, followed in seconds by a huge explosion that vibrated through the ship. In the heat of the moment the aircrew had failed to jettison their depth charges before ditching. The charges were armed ready to attack submerging U-boats, and set to explode at fifty to one hundred feet down.

Hill stripped off his clothes, handed them to an astonished stoker, dived over the side and headed for the airman farthest distant. He reached the man, *'who did not look too good to me'*, and started towing him back to the ship, which now looked a fair way off. Hill was not the only crewman to dive off the destroyer, and halfway back met a young officer cadet whom he had recently recommended for promotion. The cadet employed an immaculate breaststroke, and, displaying his best Oxbridge stiff upper lip, said, *'I have a line here sir, should you wish to use it'*.

*'Give me the bloody end'*, replied Hill, and tied a bowline around his chest. Given the word by the boatswain, seamen aboard *Ledbury*

pulled him and the injured airman in with such enthusiasm that the Captain's head contacted the ship's side with a resounding thud.

All nine of the aircrew were picked up, but despite the best efforts of the destroyer's medical team, eight of them died as a result of the explosion. They were buried at sea[8].

# III

Of the four aircraft carriers with the *Pedestal* escort, three were for convoy defence and under the command of Rear Admiral Arthur L. St. George Lyster; the fourth, *Furious*, was to fly off Spitfire reinforcements to Malta as soon as they were in range. Since this was the first occasion on which the Royal Navy had brought together so many carriers for one operation, Lyster instituted an exercise, code-named *Berserk*, which was carried out on 5 August to work up his carriers *Victorious* (flagship), *Indomitable*, and *Eagle*, into a mutually supportive fighting unit. *Berserk* entailed a searching series of manoeuvres designed to stretch both ships and aircraft to their limits and establish the roles that the individual carriers were to perform. The elderly *Argus*, purchased by the Royal Navy while under construction as a merchantman in 1916 and completed as an aircraft carrier, accompanied the convoy as far as the Bay of Biscay to assist with the exercise. Since *Victorious* had a higher proportion of the older Fulmar fighters, these would give low altitude cover, while the Martlets and Sea Hurricanes of *Indomitable* and *Eagle* would provide a high altitude fighter umbrella. Many of the aircrew involved lacked combat training and the exercises proved invaluable, although *Victorious* lost one pilot and aircraft in an unfortunate accident. A negative side effect may have been the increased radio traffic, which might well have given Axis intelligence warning that a major operation was in progress. The various types of aircraft in use were also flown slowly over the convoy to aid recognition by gunners on the merchantmen, and hopefully reduce losses from 'friendly fire'.

★   ★   ★   ★

Perhaps coincidentally, by piecing together bits and pieces of information, beginning with the less than total secrecy achieved for *Pedestal* on the Clyde, perhaps as a result of the already mentioned radio traffic, on that same 5 August, *Supermarina*, headquarters of the Italian Navy in Rome, came to the conclusion that a large British naval operation was in progress and very probably headed their way, in which case Malta would be the likely destination. Due to fuel shortages *Supermarina* would be unable to deploy its battleships, but in anticipation of more concrete intelligence, a five-point plan was drawn up to be put into operation in the event the British fleet should break into the Mediterranean. The plan involved:

1. Deployment of Italian submarines and German U-boats along the likely enemy route from the Balearic Islands to Tunisia.

2. A group of submarines to concentrate north-west of Cape Bon, to operate in conjunction with bombing missions planned for that area.

3. Temporary minefields to be laid in the anticipated route off Cape Bon (up to now not mined as Italian convoys to and from Libya used the same area).

4. Twelve Italian MAS torpedo boats, and several of the similar German E-boats, to be concentrated between Cape Bon and Pantelleria.

5. Three heavy cruisers from the 3rd Division, three light cruisers from the 7th Division, plus eleven destroyers to be placed so as to engage any surviving ships that might attempt to break through to Malta[9].

These naval dispositions were to be combined with heavy air attacks from Sardinia, Sicily, and other air bases as and when they came within range. The object of the plan was for submarines, torpedo boats and air attacks to break up the enemy formation, while the cruisers completed their destruction in detail. Given the inability to bring into play the heavy guns of their battleships, it was good strategy, and made excellent use of the restricted area that the British ships would have in which to manoeuvre. Nevertheless, the chances were that all five elements of the *Supermarina* operation would need to work in order to obtain the hoped-for total destruction of their enemy.

Although Spain remained officially neutral, the sympathies of the

1. Both the Allied and Axis High Commands realised that with the fall of France, Malta became the key to the Mediterranean and North African theatres. As a result the island became one of the most intensively bombed areas in the world. *(Photo: IWM GM 1186)*

2. General (later Field Marshal) Lord Gort, VC, replaced General Dobbie as Governor of Malta in May 1942. Refusing petrol-driven transport to encourage the conservation of vital fuel stocks, he was often to be seen cycling through the bomb-scarred streets of Valetta. *(Photo: IWM GM 1367)*

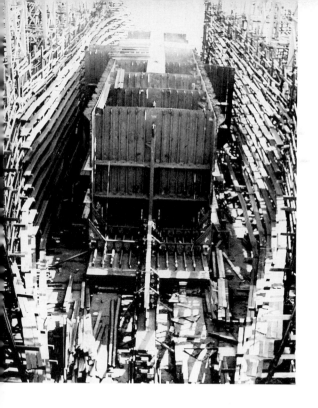

3. Hull No. 190, Slipway No. 2, Sun Shipbuilding & Drydock Co., Chester, Pennsylvania. An early stage in the constuction of *Ohio* with hull framing and the box section for the centre tanks taking shape.
*(Photo: Reproduced with the permission of Chevron USA Inc.)*

4. As she nears completion, the graceful lines of the tanker's hull are clearly visible.
*Photo: Reproduced with the permission of Chevron USA Inc.)*

5. 20th April 1940 and Mrs. Florence E. Rogers, mother of the President of The Texas Company, Mr. W.S.S. Rogers, prepares to launch the latest addition to the company's fleet. The family hailed from Ohio, hence the name for the new ship.

*(Photo: Reproduced with the permission of Chevron USA Inc.)*

6 . With the launch successfully completed, busy tugs fuss around the big new tanker and shift her to a nearby quay for fitting out.

*(Photo: Reproduced with the permission of Chevron USA Inc.)*

7. *Ohio* on trials enters the measured mile 'with a bone in her teeth'.

(Photo: Reproduced with the permission of Chevron USA Inc.)

8. *Ohio* as she would have appeared during the *Pedestal* convoy, in wartime battleship grey camouflage. (*Photo: The Mariners' Museum, Newport News, VA.*)

9. Rear-Admiral
   H.M. Burrough,
   CB, DSO, in
   command of
   force 'X', the
   *Pedestal* escort
   from Cape Bon
   to Malta.
   (*Photo: IWM 20779*)

10. 'Fiji' class cruiser. Both *Kenya* and Admiral Burrough's flagship *Nigeria* were of this
    type.
    (*Photo: IWMTA11310*)

1. Captain Dudley William Mason, GC, Master of *Ohio* for the *Pedestal* Convoy.
(*Photo: IWM HU 43092*)

12. James Wyld, DSO, Chief Engineer, *Ohio*.
(*Photo: Lafayette Ltd.*)

3. Ray Morton in 1944/45, having signed T124X Articles, hence the Royal Navy cap.
(*Photo: Ray Morton*)

14. Allan Shaw, pictured in 1942.
(*Photo: Allan Shaw*)

15. HM destroyer *Penn* in company with the battleship *Rodney*.     (*Photo: IWM A9682*)

16. Field Marshal Albert Kesselring *(left)* discusses the situation in the Western Desert with Field Marshal Erwin Rommel.
     (*Photo: IWM FLM 1434*)

17. A dramatic photograph of *Ohio* taken as she is hit by a torpedo from the Italian submarine *Axum*.

(*Photo: IWM HU 4760*)

18. Lieutenant
    Commander
    Roger Hill,
    DSO, DSM.
    (*Photo: Mr & Mrs
    N. Welby*)

19. Type 11 'Hunt' class destroyer HMS *Ledbury*. (*Photo: IWM A30687*)

20. The 'Dido' class cruiser HMS *Charybdis* engages German and Italian torpedo
    boats during the night of 12/13 August. (*Photo: IWM A11247*)

21. An Italian MAS torpedo boat of the type that attacked *Pedestal* to such devastating
    effect under cover of dark. (*Photo: IWM HU 43228*)

22. The exceptionally versatile Junkers Ju88 fighter/bomber, used in a variety of roles against *Pedestal*. *(Photo: IWM MH 6115)*

23. The Junkers Ju87 'Stuka' dive-bomber. One of the most successful anti-shipping aircraft of the war. *(Photo: IWM MH 11553)*

24. The freighter *Dorset* under heavy air attack.  (*Photo: IWM A11173*)

25. Type 11 'Hunt' class destroyer HMS *Bramham*.  (*Photo: IWM A12072*)

26. Her engines dead, her hull practically broken in two, *Ohio* is nudged gingerly along the swept channel between minefields...

(*Photo: IWM A11261*)

27. ...and into Grand Harbour.

(*Photo: IWM FLM 3441*)

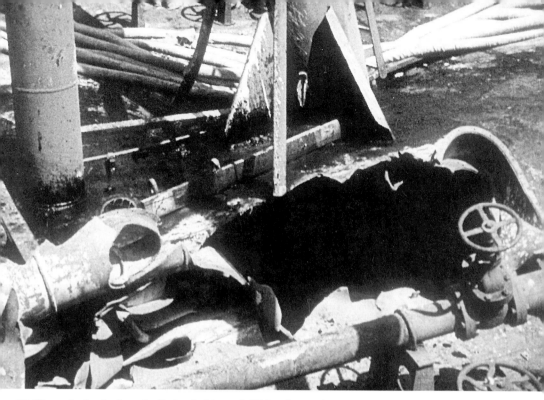

28. Torn deck plating abaft the bridge of *Ohio*, above the pump room where the torpedo from *Axum* struck home.    (*Photo: IWM FLM 3442*)

29. The crew of *Ohio* takes a well-earned break on Malta following their epic voyage.    (*Photo: IWM FLM 3443*)

30. Docked at last in Grand Harbour, *Rochester Castle* discharges her invaluable cargo.
*(Photo: IWM A11308)*

31. Dry-docked in Malta, bomb damage to *Ohio* in the shape of a gaping hole in her hull in way of the engine room is revealed. Dockyard workers expressed astonishment that the ship arrived in Grand Harbour at all.
*(Photo: National Petroleum News)*

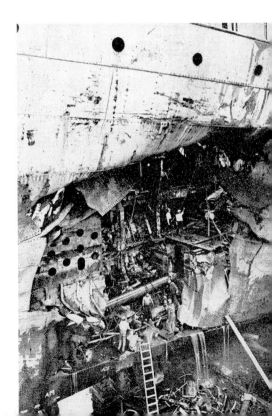

Franco dictatorship in Madrid were not unnaturally pro-fascist. The German *Abwehr* (Secret Service), taking advantage of this climate of semi-official tolerance, established a highly effective network of agents in Spain, particularly around Gibraltar, and notably in Algeciras, from where it was possible to record Allied naval comings and goings in Gibraltar across the bay. Being neutral, and close to Gibraltar, Algeciras was also a place where Allied and Axis naval personnel might mingle, raising all the possibilities that circumstance would inevitably bring for espionage by both sides.

The *Abwehr* also took advantage of the fact that many Spaniards worked in Gibraltar, crossing the border to The Rock in the morning and returning to Spain in the evening. Locals sympathetic to the fascist cause would be recruited and filtered through with the workers, to return with much valuable information concerning enemy naval movements. *Abwehr* agents also targeted local fishing fleets. With their distinctive local boats spending long periods strung out across the Straits between Spain and Algeria, fishermen could hardly fail to notice shipping passing to and fro and were ideally placed to gather much detailed intelligence.

As the amount of information reaching Berlin concerning the approaching convoy grew, it was relayed to Field Marshal Kesselring, who combined with his Italian opposite number to organise a detailed German/Italian operation closely based on the Italian five-point plan already mentioned. All was not sweetness and light between the Axis partners however, as Kesselring harboured serious doubts as to the ability of the Italian cruisers to complete the task assigned to them.

★　　★　　★　　★

*Pedestal* approached the Straits of Gibraltar so as to pass through during the night of 9/10 August. However, a complicated series of refuelling operations were necessary, particularly for the relatively short-range destroyers. Although some warships were fitted for re-fuelling at sea, the problems inherent in refuelling a large number of ships in a short space of time were exacerbated by Royal Navy indifference in the pre-war years to the most up to date techniques, and an unseemly 'queue' developed at the Gibraltar oil terminals. Almost inevitably a certain amount of confusion arose, resulting in the carrier *Indomitable* and the cruiser *Manchester* being obliged to enter Gibraltar twice to fill their bunker tanks to capacity.

While warships dashed to and from Gibraltar, the merchantmen had no fuel problems and manoeuvred into two-column formation to pass through the Straits, which they did in the early hours of the 10th. Despite making the passage at night and in a fortuitous fog, Spanish fishing boats were present in some numbers, their flickering naphtha flares showing a ghostly incandescence in the mist. Crewmen aboard the freighter *Santa Elisa* had the unnerving experience of overhearing an enemy transmission in which the merchant vessels comprising *Pedestal* were mentioned by name[10].

Dawn of 10 August broke bright and clear, with a warm sunny summer day in prospect. The grey-green of the Atlantic gave way to the deep blue of the Mediterranean, and many a crewman had the feeling that he might be on a holiday cruise. The merchant ships shook themselves out into their four-column formation once more, and were a bustle of orderly activity as men went about their routine chores. Aboard *Ohio*, pump man Alexander Collins, who hailed from the leafy suburbs of Surrey, found himself detailed ammunition supply man for the Bofors gun on the poop deck aft. Since it was his job to get the ammunition to the gun, it did not take him long to notice that there was no hoist with which to do it, and further to appreciate that the alternative entailed running up several companion ways carrying the shells. The enterprising seaman there-fore set about devising and constructing a hoist himself using spare piping from the ship's stores. The result bore an eerie resemblance to a gallows, and Collins thereafter gloried in the nickname 'The Hangman'[11]. The tanker's contingent of gunners from the Maritime Regiment of the Royal Artillery, under Bombardier Reginald La Bern, checked and rechecked guns and equipment and went through their paces, as did Royal Navy gunners under Gunlayer Alexander Pilling, RN.

Aboard *Ledbury*, Roger Hill felt the need to explain to his men their purpose with the convoy. It is evident that Captain Hill felt keenly recent events in the Arctic, believing that, although no blame could attach to him or his crew, *Ledbury* had somehow to expunge the memory of that disastrous operation. Calling the crew together, he went through the details of their present mission, and closed by saying *'you know what happened on PQ17; as long as there is a merchant ship afloat we shall stay with it'*. Hill was pleased to note the gruff approval of the crew, with grins all round, and felt that his command would never be in better shape for action[12].

By 10 August, Lord Gort had come to the reluctant conclusion that unless *Pedestal* could deliver a substantial quantity of supplies, his

'Target Date' for the surrender of Malta would lie between 31 August and 7 September.

At 17.00hrs that same day, a French civilian airliner en route from France to Algeria over-flew *Pedestal*, the pilot broadcasting a report of the composition, speed and direction of the convoy, noting the number of battleships, aircraft carriers, and other details. Even if Axis intelligence had not previously known the strength of the British force, they did now.

## Notes

[1] *SC88/5*, File 1, Shell Archive, Shell Centre, London.
[2] *MALTA CONVOY*, Peter Shankland & Anthony Hunter, Fontana Books, 1963, p. 82.
[3] Ray Morton, in correspondence with the author.
[4] PRO. ADM 237/270.
[5] *EAGLE FLEET*, W.E. Lucas, Weidenfeld & Nicolson, 1955, p. 74.
[6] *Op.cit.* Note 2, p. 85.
[7] Allan Shaw, in correspondence with the author.
[8] *DESTROYER CAPTAIN*, Roger Hill, Wm. Kimber, 1975, pp. 53/54.
[9] *THE ITALIAN NAVY IN WORLD WAR II*, Cdr. (R) Marc' Antonio Bragadin, United States Naval Institute, 1957, p. 207.
[10] *MALTA CONVOYS 1940-43*, Richard Woodman, John Murray (Publishers) Ltd., 2000, p. 383.
[11] *Op.cit.* Note 2, p. 87.
[12] *Op.cit.* Note 7, p. 62.

# CHAPTER FIVE

# 'TROUBLE ON
# A GRAND SCALE ...'

## I

11 August saw *Pedestal* steaming eastwards in four-column formation with escorts arranged in a protective circle (see diagram pages 58 & 59). The morning passed relatively uneventfully, and although the Italian submarine *Uarsciek* reported successfully attacking the carrier *Furious* at 04.38hrs[1], there is no mention in the British records of her being hit then, or as the result of a subsequent strike by the Italian submarine *Dagabur*. Italian sources point to the fact that she dry docked upon her return to Gibraltar as confirmation that she had in fact been damaged in one of these incidents.

For those warships suitably equipped, refuelling continued from the Fleet Oilers *Brown Ranger* and *Dingledale*, a highly complex and dangerous affair in waters known to be a hunting ground for enemy submarines. A cruiser or destroyer refuelling at sea could spend up to two hours hooked up to the tanker, during which time both ships would be 'sitting ducks'. Vice Admiral Syfret later complimented the crews of the two oilers on completing their task with extreme efficiency. At 08.00hrs the corvette *Coltsfoot*, astern of the convoy, reported two torpedoes breaking the surface, although they ran on harmlessly. Enemy reconnaissance aircraft were also in evidence during the morning, and the carriers vectored fighters aloft to intercept and keep them at a respectable distance.

Aboard *Ohio*, Ray Morton took an opportunity after lunch to relax on the after deck with a cigarette and an iced coffee. With the time approaching 13.15hrs, Ray was taking his ease on a bollard and having a pleasant chat in the warm sunshine with Mario Guidotti, the fifteen-year-old galley boy from Glasgow (who lied about his age to see some action), when, as the former Assistant Steward graphically puts it, *'constipation was cured'*. As the two watched *Eagle*, on the starboard quarter of the convoy, four huge spouts of water shot up along the carrier's port side, followed by the dull thud of underwater explosions. Allan Shaw remembers having just finished lunch when the carrier was hit, *'and we had trouble on a grand scale.'*

Assigned electrician for 'X' turret, third in line of the three turrets comprising the main 16" (406mm) armament of the flagship *Nelson*, nineteen-year-old AB Torpedo Man Vic Simmons came up for a breath of fresh air. He emerged from the turret gun house to see *Eagle* struck, and watched horrified as the massive aircraft carrier tilted crazily to port, men and aircraft slipping off her flight deck into the sea. The young Able Seaman's best friend served aboard *Eagle*, and it was some time before Vic learned that he was one of 862 ratings and sixty-seven officers rescued from a total complement of 1,160[2].

*Eagle* turned turtle and sank within ten minutes as the result of a highly skilled attack by *U73*, a German Type VIIB U-boat under the command of *Kapitänleutnant* Helmut Rosenbaum. The U-boat stalked the convoy for close to two hours before being able to slip between destroyers in the covering screen and fire a four-torpedo salvo at the target, which Rosenbaum correctly identified. It is possible that the destroyers of the escort were unable to locate the U-boat due to the phenomenon known as 'layering', to which the Western Mediterranean is prone. Cold water from the Atlantic enters the warm Mediterranean forming 'layers' of a different temperature and density. Serious disruption to Second World War submarine detection equipment would result. Whatever the cause, an early lesson had been rammed home. This would be no holiday cruise.

With *Eagle* torpedoed, Vice Admiral Syfret ordered the rest of the convoy to increase speed to 16 knots and put into operation emergency evasive action in formation, as practised so diligently in the Atlantic. Numerous submarine sightings were made, including one by *Ohio*, a lookout spotting a boat on the point of surfacing on the starboard beam[3]. The 5" (127mm) low angle gun aft was brought to bear, but unable to go into action as the submarine immediately dived, and other ships were close to the line of fire.

Later that afternoon *Furious* flew off her reinforcement of thirty-seven Spitfires for Malta, during which *Nelson* and *Rodney* threw up a brief radar-controlled barrage from their 16" (406mm) guns to deter

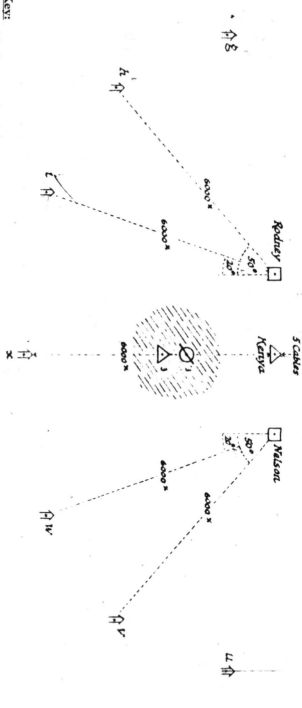

**Key:**

m = guide destroyer for the advance screen.

m, a, b, c, d and m, o, p, q, r, s = advance screen destroyers 2000 yards/1829m apart.

f, g, t, u = wing destroyers 3000 yards/2743m apart

j,k,l,n = 'Hunt' class destroyers 600 yards/548m clear of the wing columns of merchantmen.

3 = aircraft carriers plus attendant cruisers.

6000x = 6000 yards/5486m.

z = the tug *Jaunty*.

Columns of merchantmen 5 cables (1690 yards/1545m) apart.

Diagram: PRO.ADM 199/1243.

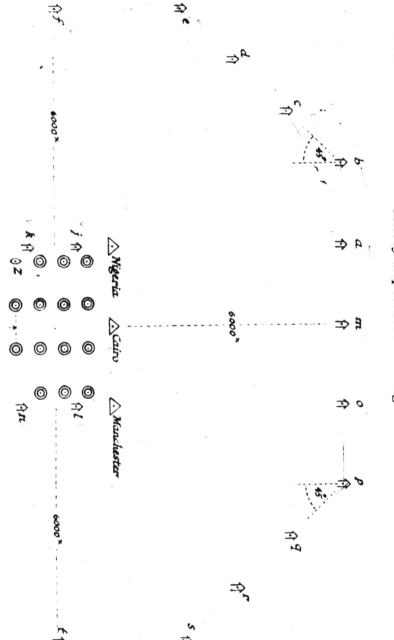

Convoy dispositions ~ 11 August

enemy reconnaissance aircraft reported in the area. For additional anti-aircraft fire, the battleships were equipped with short-fuse ammunition for their main armament, the anticipated effect being that the detonation from each 16" (406mm) shell would clear a square mile of sky. Allan Shaw still has vivid memories of the smell of burnt cordite drifting across the columns of ships as the big battlewagons opened up. Having successfully completed the first part of her task (she was to pick up another load of thirty-plus Spitfires for Malta), *Furious* turned back for Gibraltar with a destroyer escort and the *Jaunty*, the deck of the latter crammed with survivors from *Eagle*. Despite her anticipated speed of 15 knots proving to be optimistic, it was nevertheless a costly miscalculation to detach her from the convoy at this early stage. The presence of a tug in the days to come would have been priceless, as events were soon to show.

★　　★　　★　　★

The hot day cooled into evening and at 18.45hrs, from the Italian port of Trapani the 'Adua' class submarine *Axum*, captained by Lieutenant Commander Renato Ferrini, slipped her moorings and headed out into the Central Mediterranean to join her hunting group lying in wait for the Allied ships north-west of Cape Bon[4].

★　　★　　★　　★

Sunset on the 11th came at 20.40hrs, and approximately a quarter of an hour later bombers were homing in on the convoy. Destroyers on the outer ring opened fire first, followed by cruisers, battleships and merchantmen, until the cacophony of ack-ack fire was deafening. *Victorious* and *Indomitable* scrambled fighters into the air, and a series of jumbled dogfights ensued in the deepening dusk. These initial attacks, carried out by bombers and torpedo aircraft from Luftwaffe *Kampfgruppen* 54 and 77 based in Sicily[5], were to probe convoy defences and seek out the carriers as their main objectives, *Victorious* in particular being forced to take drastic evasive action as sticks of bombs fell close around her. No determined effort was made against the merchantmen however, and Lieutenant Barton reported that no bombs fell closer to *Ohio* than about three cables (approximately 600 yards/549m). The anti-aircraft cruiser *Cairo* brought down a Ju88 with her first salvo, and one, possibly two more Ju88s were shot down on the port side of the convoy.

60

Captain Mason reported that the day had seemed '*full of emergency turns and salvos of depth charges*', and that for *Ohio* the night passed without disturbance, gunners asleep at their posts and all hands ready for any emergency, the majority sleeping on deck.

# II

By 06.00hrs on 12 August, the dawn glow on the eastern horizon had already brightened into another dazzling Mediterranean summer day. *Axum* cruised her patrol area and received orders to submerge and await reconnaissance reports on the enemy's position. Lieutenant Commander Ferrini took his boat to periscope depth and kept watch to westward for telltale smudges of smoke heralding the approach of the convoy. Strung out along *Pedestal*'s line of advance were *Axum*'s sister vessel *Dessie* (Lieutenant Commander Renato Scandolo), six more Italian submarines and several German U-boats.

On the airfields of Sardinia and Sicily, German and Italian ground crew went through their well-ordered routines for fuelling and arming the bombers, torpedo planes and fighters parked in neat rows along-side the runways. Here and there wreckage remained to be cleared away from the previous night's raids. During August, airfields on both Sardinia and Sicily were subject to regular attack by the small number of Beauforts and Beaufighters available in Malta, and nerves were taut. At 08.00hrs, two Ju88s, with their similar twin-engine profile to the Bristol-built aircraft, overflew Sardinia and were mistakenly shot down by Italian fighters.

Despite the raids, an estimated 540 aircraft remained available to the Axis military command, including 150 Luftwaffe bombers and torpedo aircraft with fifty fighters in support, augmented by 130 bombers and torpedo aircraft of the *Regia Aeronautica* with 150 fighters in support, the remainder comprising reconnaissance and support aircraft. In a coordinated series of attacks, wave after wave of aircraft were to be launched against the convoy, and as each wave returned to base to be succeeded by the next attack, aircrew were to be rested before flying another mission.

Destruction of the merchant ships was now the prime Axis objective, and the gunners and crews of the *Pedestal* ships would have no opportunity to rest. They would have to remain at their action stations until the attacks stopped or they entered Grand Harbour.

★　★　★　★

At first light, a Ju88 of Luftwaffe Reconnaissance Group 122, and a Cant Z 1007/bis from 212 Squadron, *Regia Aeronautica*, approached the convoy, and fighters from *Victorious* and *Indomitable* were soon airborne and in pursuit. The interlopers could not be caught however, and valuable information was gained concerning position, course and speed of the ships. Submarines were also suspected, and at 07.41hrs, astern of the convoy, the cruiser *Kenya* was forced to put her helm hard over in order to 'comb' torpedo tracks. Destroyers sped to the scene of a suspected submarine echo but were soon recalled, maintenance of the protective screen around the merchantmen being more important than hunting down what might or might not prove to be an enemy. At 09.00hrs, Ju88s of KG54 and KG77, nineteen in number, returned to deliver a high-level bombing attack, and, in the face of a furious barrage from the convoy, failed to score any hits. Alarms warning of aircraft and submarines now came in thick and fast and emergency turns, first to port then to starboard seemed to come every few minutes. Destroyers continued to chase suspected submarine echoes, but being unable to linger too far from the screen were unable to register a 'kill'. They were, however, able to force the abandonment of more than one attacking run by Axis boats.

The day wore on towards noon and aboard *Ohio* gun crews remained at their posts awaiting the next attack. Ahead, destroyers on the outer screen opened fire on approaching aircraft, puffs of smoke appearing in the clear bright blue summer sky and increasing in intensity, followed by the booming of gunfire like the distant rumbling thunder of an approaching summer storm. The *Regia Aeronautica* now mounted a three-pronged assault designed to overwhelm the convoy defences; however, with differing departure points and distances to their target, attacking aircraft came in as three distinct waves, rather than elements of the same attack. The first wave, which the destroyers now engaged, comprised five SM84 bombers from 32 Land Bomber Formation, plus five SM84s from 32 Torpedo Bomber Formation, which dropped Italian-designed *motobomba* mines by parachute. On hitting the water an automatic pressure device operated a compressed-air-driven propeller and drove the *motobombas* around in circles of some fifteen kilometres radius, the intention being to break up the convoy formation as much as to hit anything with the mines themselves. Syfret ordered an immediate turn to port followed by a return to the mean course some minutes later.

During these manoeuvres, the second wave, twelve SM79s of 2 and 3 Torpedo Bomber Units, plus ten SM84s of 32 Formation, were to make torpedo attacks supported by nine SM79s of 130 Torpedo Bomber Group, augmented by fifteen obsolete CR42 biplanes, which were to make machine-gun attacks to draw enemy fire. Twenty-six Re2001 fighters from the 2/362 Land Fighter Squadrons would provide cover, plus fourteen Mc202s from 153 Land Fighter Group. Due to the late arrival of these formations, fighters from *Victorious* and *Indomitable* were able to intercept and break up their attack; nevertheless several Italian aircraft pressed home their assault but ran into an intense curtain of anti-aircraft fire from the ships, including a splash barrage* from *Rodney's* 16" (406mm) guns, and again the Axis aircraft were driven off. No hits on the convoy were reported. As the Italian aircraft withdrew, the third wave, thirty-seven Ju88s from KG 54 and 77, arrived over the convoy and commenced their attack. Defending fighters attempted to break up the formations, and ships' gunners again put up a ferocious barrage. Nevertheless, twelve aircraft broke through the defensive cordon and swept across the convoy from starboard to port at around 3,000 feet, (914m), bombs from this attack near-missing both battleships and the cruiser *Cairo*. The merchantmen experienced their first casualty when *Deucalion*, leading the port outer column, was first near-missed, then hit squarely in No.5 hold. The freighter suffered serious damage but her master, Captain Brown, believed she might still make Malta, and accompanied by the destroyer *Bramham* left the convoy to make for the inshore route along the Tunisian coast, at a much-reduced 8 knots.

'*Snatch a meal whenever you can, let a lifejacket become part of the 'garb'* . . . *all hell breaking loose and all jobs were done automatically*' – to Allan Shaw, assisting the *Ohio* gunners, the attacks seemed unending – '*two of us were passing ammo to the gun crew . . . keeping one of the Oerlikon guns going by reloading the "pans" full of bullets. Changing the empty pans and getting full ones was down to a fine art and only took a few seconds, so while the guns were firing we were pretty busy . . . We could see tracer hitting the planes, but the pace was so hectic you didn't see what happened to the ones hit because another three or four were heading for us . . . The barrage from all the ships had to be seen to be believed*'. And all the while the indescribable din of bomb bursts and anti-aircraft fire. But, even in the

---

* Designed to raise a curtain of water ahead of low flying torpedo bombers to break up their attacks.

afternoon sunshine, the rose-coloured tracer and delicately tinted pompom shells arcing high into the sky could seem *'ludicrously like a peacetime firework display'*[6].

As the holder of an AA gunner's ticket, Ray Morton manned a light machine gun situated port side on the tanker's after boat deck, and remembers *'the severity and continuity of the air attacks was ferocious with a capital F. You just stayed at action stations – you didn't have time for anything and you didn't sleep. Wherever you pointed the gun there was an enemy plane and you just kept pulling the trigger . . . The sky was like a huge lace curtain with the shell bursts from close to a hundred ships and it just stayed that way. Bombs were raining down and planes were falling out of the sky . . . Near misses were two a penny'.* During a brief respite, Ray heard Mario Guidotti ask plaintively, *'Is it always like this?'*

*'Oh no'*, came the reply, *'it gets wilder yet!'*

As these attacks died away the *Regia Aeronautica* launched two more strikes, one that demonstrated the often-underrated technical ingenuity of the Italian armed forces, the other once again demonstrating their brio in 'guerrilla' style operations. It is often assumed that the first unmanned flying-bomb was the German V1; however by 1942 the *Regia Aeronautica* had developed a radio-controlled SM79 bomber which, loaded with a 630lb (286kg) armour-piercing bomb, was taken to operational altitude by a pilot who then baled out. Control by radio then passed to an accompanying aircraft, for *Pedestal* a Cant Z1007b11, which, from a safe distance, was to guide the 'flying bomb' on to either a carrier or battleship. Damage, should the attack have been successful, would have been enormous, possibly fatal. Fortunately for the convoy, a fault developed in the radio-control equipment and the unmanned SM79 droned on until it ran out of fuel and crashed on the Algerian mainland – much to the consternation of the Vichy French authorities[7].

The second strike was, if anything, even more audacious, although with less potential for serious damage, and involved the pilots of two Re2001 fighters from the G.V. (Special Operations) Section, equipped with 100lb (45kg) bombs, attaching themselves to the end of a line of Sea Hurricanes circling *Victorious* awaiting their turn to land. The two Italian pilots also coolly awaited their opportunity then detached themselves from the Hurricanes and swooped in low over the carrier – unopposed, since it was assumed that two of the Hurricane pilots were putting on a show of youthful exuberance. The Re2001's dropped their bombs and screamed away pursued by streams of ack-ack fire from suddenly awakened gunners. Again luck was not with the *Regia Aeronautica* as the first bomb broke up on impact with *Victorious* armoured flight deck, while the second exploded harmlessly as it dropped off her bow. However, both Italian aircraft made good their escape.

As the Axis aircraft withdrew, Italian and German submarines, circling the convoy like hungry sharks, probed for weaknesses. Attacks were made and beaten off, emergency turns made this way and that, and all punctuated by the thud of exploding depth charges as the destroyers attempted to maintain their defensive screen. The Italian submarine *Cobalto,* discovered and subjected to fierce depth charge attack, was first damaged and then forced to the surface, where she was rammed and sunk by the destroyer *Ithuriel.*

★  ★  ★  ★

Surfaced some way ahead of the convoy, Lieutenant Commander Ferrini studied incoming intelligence reports and came to the conclusion that he was too far south and east of his ideal position. *Axum* slipped beneath the warm Mediterranean waters and Ferrini took her on to course 330° to close with his intended targets. He surfaced in position 37°37' Longitude, 10°21' Latitude to await a sighting to westward, and by 16.21hrs had visual contact at extreme range on what he believed to be a large cargo vessel or aircraft carrier. *Axum* again submerged, and Ferrini began his approach to establish the identity of this possible target.

# III

As 12 August drew on towards evening, the convoy neared the latitude of Cape Bon and the point at which the carriers and heavy ships of the escort would turn back for Gibraltar, leaving Burrough's Force X to take the merchantmen through the Narrows. The Axis High Command, who believed this to be the pivotal stage of the engagement, foresaw the division of the escort and planned an intense series of air attacks designed to exact a heavy toll on the convoy and Force X, and inflict as much damage upon Syfret's fleet as possible before it could pull back out of range of aircraft based on Sicily and Sardinia. Crippled warships and merchantmen would be finished off by submarines the following morning, while Italian cruisers mopped up what was left of *Pedestal* as it attempted to reach Malta.

Syfret came to the conclusion that the moment for his ships to turn back would be 19.15hrs, enabling him to offer the protection of his aircraft and heavy ships for as long as possible, finally leaving the convoy to make its way through the Narrows under cover of darkness. However, approaching 17.45hrs, numbers of Axis aircraft were located on radar, gathering at various points around the convoy. These were twenty-nine Luftwaffe Ju87 Stuka dive-bombers (highly effective anti-ship aircraft) of Stukageschwader 3, supported by CR42s, plus nine *Regia Aeronautica* Stukas from 102 Group, and fourteen SM79 torpedo bombers from 132 Torpedo Bomber Group. Due to damage, losses and repairs, fighter support was becoming a problem for the *Regia Aeronautica* (and would become a highly contentious issue in the days to come); however, a number of Mc202s, Re2001s, and the obsolete CR42s were scraped together, while the Luftwaffe supplied Me109s and Me110s from Jagdgruppe 53 to support its own Stukas.

At around 17.50, four Stukas attacked the damaged *Ithuriel*, some way astern after picking up survivors from *Cobalto*. She beat them off and hurried at her best speed, now down to 20 knots, to catch up with the main body. The carriers had fighters aloft and dogfights flared up around the convoy, which altered course to east-south-east and made for the Narrows. Axis aircraft were now in plain sight, SM79 torpedo bombers attacking from the south while Italian Stukas pounced on *Rodney*, near-missing the battleship but losing two of their number. The convoy took avoiding action and *Indomitable* found herself attacked by twelve Luftwaffe Stukas swooping down out of the setting sun. Positioned astern of *Rodney* on the port quarter of the convoy, her anti-aircraft cruiser *Phoebe* fully engaged by a group of SM79s attempting to work their way astern, *Indomitable* was vulnerable, and experienced German aircrew spotted the opening. Diving from 12,000 feet (3,657m), at what appeared to observers to be an angle of 50°, a number of these courageous and highly skilled pilots brought their machines down to 1,000 feet (305m) before releasing their bombs, so intent were they on scoring hits. Quickly straddled, the carrier disappeared behind columns of water as she took evasive action. A Stuka dived in for a bombing run and flew the length of the ship, three bombs exploding on her after flight deck, wrecking it. Almost immediately, on the outer screen, SM79s torpedoed the destroyer *Foresight*, the explosion blowing away her stern. On the flagship *Nelson,* Vic Simmons emerged from X turret to see *Indomitable* hit and *'I decided then to stay in the gun house – each time I went on top something dreadful happened'.*

Fires raged aboard *Indomitable,* but thanks to the Royal Navy practice of building aircraft carriers with armoured flight decks she was saved from destruction. However, with her flight deck destroyed she was of no further practical use, and all her aircraft then airborne were diverted to *Victorious.* Having again failed to get through to the merchantmen, the Axis aircraft gradually withdrew. However, as a result of the damage to *Indomitable,* and other casualties, Vice Admiral Syfret moved the time for his withdrawal up to 18.55hrs, and wishing the convoy 'God Speed' turned his ships back to Gibraltar.

★   ★   ★   ★

Despite having encountered determined air and submarine attacks, and thanks in large measure to the heavily outnumbered pilots of the Fleet Air Arm, the convoy remained in good shape with only one merchantman, *Deucalion* damaged, but still plodding determinedly along the Algerian coast accompanied by *Bramham* (replaced in Force X by the destroyer *Wilton*).

However, to pass through the Narrows the main body would necessarily have to alter the four-column formation to two, (see diagram page 69). With the opportunity to practice on the way down to Gibraltar, the masters of the merchant ships had proven themselves adept at these manoeuvres, and Burrough entertained no great misgivings concerning the deployment. Nevertheless, the convoy would undoubtedly encounter further air attacks, and an hour or two would be taken to make the change; consequently the Rear Admiral gave the order as soon as Syfret's ships turned to westward.

It had been Syfret's intention for aircraft from his carriers to cover the convoy until nightfall, but with *Indomitable* out of action and *Victorious* consequently crowded with aircraft in various stages of rearmament, refuelling or repair, inevitable delays occurred. In fact, aboard the one remaining operational carrier, such was the premium on time and deck space that damaged aircraft, which in other circumstances would have been deemed repairable, were pitched over the side.

By 19.38hrs, Lieutenant Commander Scandolo had worked his submarine *Dessie* into a position north-east of the convoy, and from a distance of approximately one mile launched a four-torpedo salvo, all of which missed their mark, but crucially their tracks were not seen by the escort, concentrating as they were on the ever-present bombers and therefore unaware of the close proximity of submarines as the convoy continued its change of formation.

At 19.27hrs, in position 37°37' Latitude, 10°19' Longitude, Lieutenant Commander Ferrini brought *Axum* up to periscope depth for a better look at his targets, now some 8,750 yards (8,000 metres) to the south-west, and in so doing gained his first clear look at the convoy. Turning to a parallel course in order to study his quarry, Ferrini established a close estimate of the number of cargo ships and escorts that he faced, and by 19.37hrs had closed his boat to approximately 4,375 yards (4,000 metres). Taken down to fifty feet (fifteen metres), *Axum* worked in closer and at 19.48hrs her captain brought her up to periscope depth to take another look. Almost filling his viewfinder, a large cruiser led a merchant vessel in the line nearest the submarine, while beyond this steamed a second line of ships. Ferrini had adroitly presented himself with every submarine commander's dream – an almost unmissable target. At 19.55hrs, with distance to the cruiser down to 1,421 yards (1300m), he launched a salvo of four torpedoes from the bow tubes in the order one – four – three – two, instructing that one and two be set to run straight, while four and three should be angled 5° to port and starboard respectively.

# IV

To effect the change from four columns into two, the plan was for the port inner column of merchantmen to drop astern of the port outer column, and the starboard outer column astern of the starboard inner column. For the resulting two-column formation the port and starboard columns were to be headed by the cruisers *Nigeria* and *Manchester* respectively. Fourth in line behind *Nigeria* would be the anti-aircraft cruiser *Cairo*, and fifth behind *Manchester* the cruiser *Kenya*. Force X destroyers were to form a screen around the whole. With these manoeuvres well under way, *Nigeria* headed the port column, *Cairo* dropped back to take position, and *Ohio* maintained station astern of *Empire Hope* in the starboard column. At 19.56hrs, Ferrini's first torpedo hit Burrough's flagship *Nigeria* port side under the bridge superstructure, and *Pedestal*'s world turned upside down. From *Empire Hope*, on station at the forward end of the starboard line,

68

***Two-column formation
intended but never
actually achieved for
passage through The
Narrows.***

**Key:**

g,h,s,t = minesweeping
(T.S.D.S.) destroyers.

c, w = rescue destroyers.

Columns of merchantmen
to be five cables (1,690
yards/1,545m) apart,
ships in column to be
three cables (1,013
yards/927m) apart.

Remaining destroyers to
tuck in closely on either
side of the convoy.

Diagram taken from
Admiral Burrough's orig-
inal plan. By the time the
two-column formation
was attempted, ship
No.11, *Deucalion,* and the
tug *Jaunty,* were no
longer with the main body
of the convoy.

Diagram: PRO.ADM
199/1243.

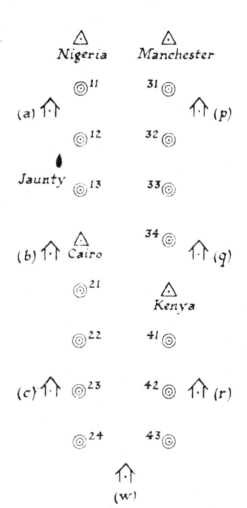

seaman Jim Perry watched *Cairo 'firing like mad to starboard . . . which meant torpedo bombers making for her. Ours and other ships guns were blazing away when the stern of the cruiser just exploded . . . bits of plating seemed to be just slowly turning over and over before coming down like burnt paper from a bonfire . . . '*[8]. While engaging aircraft to starboard, *Cairo* was hit portside aft by two of *Axum's* torpedoes. Aboard the stricken anti-aircraft cruiser, *Daily Express* war correspondent Norman Smart picked himself up from the deck, looked to starboard and saw the fourth torpedo strike *Ohio* port side amidships.

The torpedo hit the tanker's pump room abaft the bridge super-structure, blew a hole 24 feet by 27 feet (7.32m x 8.23m) in the ship's side, tore a gaping hole in her deck plating, and caused a huge fire in the port side wing tanks, loaded with kerosene. All things being equal, that should have been the death blow for *Ohio* and her highly volatile cargo. The vessel heeled over, shook violently, and a searing ball of smoke and flame roared skywards. Initially, Captain Mason must have considered the ship finished, and ordered the crew mustered at their boat stations. However, it quickly became apparent that while the conflagration was bad enough, it was not getting any worse, and Mason had a five-man fire party, including Chief Officer Douglas Gray, Chief Steward Francis Meeks, Pump Man Robert Watson and Carpenter Robert Horton, fight the fire with Foamite extinguishers. Assisted by the massive inrush of seawater, they had the fire out in about five minutes, and an inspection of the damage revealed a tear in the deck plating extending as far as the centreline bulkhead and down some 5 feet (1.5m) into the pump room bulkheads. A trail of kerosene leaked into the sea from the ship's port side wing tanks, most of the lids having been blown open and buckled. The pump room was open to the sea, gyrocompass out of action, steering from the bridge no longer possible (telemotor piping along the deck had been torn apart by the blast), and communication with the aft end of the ship, including the engine room, virtually cut. Mercifully, there was one exception to the communications blackout – the telephone. The explosion also blew shell plating outwards in way of the pump room, these buckled and twisted plates now having the same effect as a rudder and dragging *Ohio* round in a circle to port. Mason ordered engines stopped as the ship was a danger to others in the convoy, many of which were forced to take evasive action in order to avoid a colli-sion[9].

Amid continuing air attacks, Allan Shaw found himself sent aft with Chief Officer Gray to connect steering via the direct steam steering

70

position on the poop deck abaft the funnel. He remembers *'the deck jumping up and down in the steering flat'* as bombs near-missed the ship, and that *'trying to rig emergency steering gear in these conditions was something unusual . . . after a while when things eased off, the silence was eerie, wondering what's next. Grab a cup of coffee while you can, a trip to the cabin to roll a few fags and back on deck to see what's going on . . . '*

Mason asked James Wyld if it would be possible to get under way again. However, on returning to the engine room, Wyld and his engineers found steam practically off the boilers. The Chief Engineer sent several engineers and an electrician to start the diesel generator, had the fuel pump and forced draught fans working and raised steam to working pressure. Engines were successfully started at 20.35, and stopped again at 20.40 while Gray completed rigging steering from the aft position[10].

★   ★   ★   ★

As the torpedo hit *Ohio*, Ray Morton manned his machine gun on the boat deck. The explosion threw a geyser of kerosene and water high into the air and Ray remembers somebody slamming him forcefully against a bulkhead under a gun mounting, out of the deluge. He must have lost consciousness as the next thing he remembers, *'I was in the oggin, bobbing up and down in my life jacket complete with red light and whistle'*. *Ohio*, belching smoke and flame, steamed on her way *'without even a wave'*, but Ray soon discovered that he was not alone in that patch of the Mediterranean. When Captain Mason ordered the crew to boat stations, two army gunners, W. Hands and Eddie Smith, plus galley boy Mario Guidotti, went as far as climbing into their lifeboat, which was then tipped over, probably by a near-miss bomb blast, pitching its occupants into the sea. Ray spotted them a short distance away, but the struggling seamen also had less friendly company to contend with. Axis aircraft decided to use them for target practice and swooped low, machine-gunning them as they went. This was altogether too much for Guidotti, who yelled *'you stupid bastards, you couldn't hit a barn door!'* Ray wished Mario would be quiet in case the pilots heard him. There was of course no chance that might happen, *'it's just one of those stupid things you can think in tight situations'*[11]. Fortunately the aircraft caused no casualties.

The four crewmen were in the sea for some three hours before *Bicester*, a 'Hunt' class destroyer searching for survivors from *Nigeria*, appeared on the scene and picked up Guidotti and the gunners. She

71

then manoeuvred over to Ray and heaving lines were hurled to him, but all dropped short. Finally it dawned on him that he was supposed to swim to the lines and grab hold. *'It's no good dropping the bloody things there'*, he yelled, *'I can't swim!'* A three-badge good conduct AB on the deck of the destroyer pushed back his cap and with a broad West Country accent replied, *'Well I'll be f . . . ed, I've heard everything now!'* As *Bicester* swung round to get closer, Ray could feel the tug of her propellers dragging him under, but seeing the danger a Petty Officer on the quarterdeck tore off his uniform, dived in and helped the struggling seaman climb a rescue net up the side of the warship. As he reached the deck Ray was pulled up and supported either side by burly AB's. *'Come on son, you're OK now'*, one said. *'I know I'm OK'* he replied, pushed them away and hit the deck like a sack of spuds[12].

Taken below to rest in a hammock, the ship's doctor checked the bedraggled survivor over and prescribed a mug full of Pusser's Rum. Ray slept like a log, and on waking the following morning demanded to know why he had been 'knocked out!'[13]

★   ★   ★   ★

Immediately following the torpedo hit, *Nigeria* took on a 15° list to port, and Rear Admiral Burrough knew that in order to maintain command of the operation he would have to shift his flag to another ship. As her boiler rooms flooded, power failed aboard the cruiser and, her steering motor jammed, but with her engines still running she too began to circle to port. Burrough ordered *Ashanti* (Commander Richard Onslow, Captain [D], Sixth Destroyer Flotilla) alongside, and the destroyer started what was to prove a difficult and lengthy chase around the circling cruiser in an attempt to get in position to embark the Admiral. Finally, at 20.20hrs, Burrough and his staff reluctantly left *Nigeria* and boarded *Ashanti*. Burrough has been criticised for electing to remain aboard the destroyer which, although a Flotilla Leader, would not have the communications systems that would have existed aboard one of the remaining cruisers, *Manchester* or *Kenya*. However, in light of subsequent events it is probably just as well that he remained where he was.

With her stern blown away, *Cairo* was doomed, and with her crew taken off, was sent to the bottom by *Derwent* before the destroyer sped westward to join her 'Hunt' class sister ships *Bicester* and *Wilton* in escorting the crippled *Nigeria* back to Gibraltar.

Following his attack, Lieutenant Commander Ferrini took *Axum* down to 213 feet (65m) and prepared for the counter-attack, which began shortly thereafter with a well-targeted round of depth charges. Ferrini took the boat down to 328 feet, (100m) where he and his crew endured two hours of bombardment. At every attempt to bring *Axum* up above 260 feet (80m), the submariners would hear the 'ping' of the destroyers' sonar pulses on the hull of their craft, and the bombardment would begin again. Having stayed for as long as they dare, the destroyers above were ultimately forced to abandon the hunt and rejoin the convoy. *Axum* finally surfaced at 22.50hrs, still close to the scene of her attack. Three large vessels in flames were clearly visible, fires aboard the nearest ship illuminating the submarine. Destroyers were spotted in the distance, and Ferrini took his boat down again and left the area.

Lieutenant Commander Ferrini had delivered what must be one of the most devastating single-salvo torpedo attacks of the war. Not only did he cripple the flagship *Nigeria*, sink *Cairo*, and badly damage *Ohio*, he completely destroyed the convoy's cohesion. All three ships struck were at or near the head of their columns as the merchantmen approached the Narrows. The convoy attempted a starboard emergency turn but a number of ships were forced to take drastic evasive action to avoid collision, some taking to a northerly, some a north-westerly heading, instead of the south-easterly course that would take them past Pantelleria. Without the time or sea room in which to re-form, the convoy, instead of entering the narrow channel in two orderly columns with warships in attendance, straggled forward with little or no formation, and accompanying warships in a state of disarray. *Manchester* and *Kenya* carried on when the attack occurred, leaving most merchantmen behind, while destroyers dashed to and fro chasing submarine echoes and attempting to round up their charges.

At this critical time Rear Admiral Burrough was unable to establish any measure of control, being initially some time disembarking from his flagship, and subsequently having to utilise the less than ideal communications aboard *Ashanti*. It might be thought that was enough for the Admiral to contend with, but there was more. *Nigeria* and *Cairo* had been the designated fighter direction ships with surface to air communications and experienced fighter control officers aboard. The convoy would shortly be within range of Malta's Beaufighters but without these cruisers it would be unable to vector them, or any fighters that *Victorious* might be able to get airborne while she too was still in range, onto enemy air attacks. Air cover for the convoy would effectively be flying 'blind', and therefore at a significant disadvantage in its efforts to break up Axis attacks.

Having received news of the disaster that had overtaken *Pedestal*, Vice Admiral Syfret immediately despatched the anti-aircraft cruiser *Charybdis* and the destroyers *Lookout*, *Lightning*, and *Somali* back to reinforce Force X.

★ ★ ★ ★

While all this had been in progress, *Pedestal* lost its first merchantman, but not with the main body. At 19.40hrs, to the southwest, as *Deucalion* made her way along the Tunisian coast, she came under attack from a pair of Ju88s. Rocked by near misses, the ship carried on but came under attack again at 21.20hrs, after sunset. Two more bombers swept in and the freighter received a direct hit. Kerosene and aviation spirit in drums exploded and the aft end of the ship was soon engulfed in flame, leaving Captain Brown no option but to order her abandoned. *Bramham* approached to pick up survivors, and having convinced himself that she would sink and not fall into enemy hands, Lieutenant Baines, her commanding officer, made haste to be away as he believed Vichy French ships to be in the area. At 22.40 hrs, while making rapidly for the convoy, a bright flash was seen astern of the destroyer as *Deucalion* blew up and sank.

On boarding *Ashanti*, Rear Admiral Burrough's first act was to come alongside the nearby *Ohio*, enquiring of Captain Mason the extent of her damage and whether she would be able to proceed. On being advised that the tanker should be under way in approximately forty minutes and that they would do their best to reach Malta, Burrough suggested that if her speed was much reduced she might better proceed independently by the inshore route. The Admiral later expressed himself *'most impressed by the gallant and cool manner in which he* [Mason] *handled the situation'*[14].

If submarines stalked the merchant ships like hungry sharks, Ju88s and torpedo bombers, taking full advantage of the confused situation in which the convoy found itself, swooped like birds of prey. From the starboard side of the convoy, *Ledbury*'s radar plot tracked aircraft closing from the port bow (making their approach from east to west the aircraft would have the convoy silhouetted against the setting sun on the western horizon). Roger Hill ordered 25 knots and set course between merchant ships in an attempt to get to the engaged side and break up the attack before it got going. The speeding destroyer was nevertheless still among the merchantmen when Ju88s swept over at masthead height. The attack was pressed home with great determination, and Lieutenant Barton reported bombs falling within 100 yards (91m) of the still stationary *Ohio*. *Brisbane Star* took a torpedo hit to her bows, and although initially brought to a standstill, later got under way and made for the inshore route along the coast.

For over thirty minutes the brand new *Empire Hope* appeared to lead a charmed life as her master, Captain Gwilym Williams, skilfully steered his ship between an estimated eighteen near misses. For Jim Perry *'everything was happening so fast. Our guns seemed more urgent . . . a bomb burst just off our bow sending spray over us. I remember crouching near the ship's saloon accommodation and moving forward waiting for the next bomb . . . by moving forward I could now see over to starboard, and in time to watch a 'plane drop three bombs on a ship in the next line . . . As in a dream I watched the bombs disappear, the ship carried on. No flash, no smoke . . . then she blew up and the sea between us was covered in crazy splashes.'*

Finally *Empire Hope*'s luck ran out when a near miss tore a hole in her side and her engines stopped. The crippled ship drew more attacks until finally, at around 20.50hrs, she sustained two direct hits aft. Jim Perry again: *'I turned...aft . . . when a sheet of flame from near the stern told me we had copped it. As I rushed towards it, a scamper of boots and the second or third mate yelled at me to turn the water on* [for a fire hose delivering water under pressure]. *When I had the hose run out, he was still yelling (there was a lot of noise going on at the time) – when I yelled back that there was no bloody water coming through!'* Bomb damage had wrecked the water pumps and the two men dashed up a companionway to the boat deck. There they were given foam extinguishers and told to play them on the centre of the flames while the crew prepared to lower lifeboats. *'By then the 'planes were still near-missing us, and . . . the flames had really got a hold. The extinguishers were empty and the word was given to abandon ship. We shoved away, picking up a couple of the crew that had jumped from the stern . . . The destroyer* Penn *picked us up. It was dark by then, and as he came up to us a soft voice said "quiet everyone, put out the red light on life jackets, wounded up first". Not far from us our ship was ablaze, and one other, so it wasn't healthy to hang around. Once on board we followed the bloke in front with a hand on his shoulder and* [were] *led down below, which was full of empty shell cases. Next morning we found we had been locked in the ammunition locker from where the forward guns were fed! We slept on the open deck after that.'*

75

Miraculously, all the crew from *Empire Hope* were rescued, but the same could not be said for *Clan Ferguson*. Hit by an aerial torpedo at 21.02hrs, she suffered a gigantic explosion. From bridge to stern was soon a sheet of flame, and she was finished. Burrough's command had been hit hard and was about to be hit again. *Manchester* and *Kenya* slowed to allow the convoy to catch up, and at approximately 21.12hrs a lookout aboard *Kenya* spotted torpedo tracks and her helm was swung hard over. Three of the salvo, from the Italian submarine *Alagi*, missed, but the fourth struck the cruiser forward, shattering her bows. Damage was serious, but after shoring up the forward bulkheads she managed to maintain 25 knots.

From the bridge of *Port Chalmers*, Commodore Venables witnessed the crippling of one quarter of his charges in just over an hour. In addition, the fate of *Nigeria* was uncertain, *Cairo* sunk, *Kenya* damaged, and he had no word from Rear Admiral Burrough. Venables had *Port Chalmers* turned westward at full speed, ordering the nearby *Melbourne Star*, *Dorset* and *Almeria Lykes* to follow, which, he being the Commodore, they did. On *Ledbury* the turn was noticed and Hill chased after the errant ships, ordering them back on to course 120° (south-east). By the time *Ledbury* arrived, discussions on the bridge of both *Melbourne Star* and *Dorset* had already led their masters to decide that they could not comply with Venables' orders, and they swung back to the south-east. *Almeria Lykes* queried the order from *Ledbury*, intending to stand on for Gibraltar, but with a little persuasion she turned again to rejoin the convoy. '*We could not blame him*', Hill later commented[15], '*but he would have been a sitting duck on his own*'. *Port Chalmers* also returned to the fold, Commodore Venables later stating that it was always his intention to turn back for Malta when the attacks died down, but it would scarcely be surprising if the speed and ferocity of events during that hour or so had shaken his resolve.

★   ★   ★   ★

With the time approaching 20.45hrs, *Ohio* again got under way. Ahead, the convoy could be seen under furious air attack, and course was altered to give it a wide berth. Mason conferred with his officers and a decision was reached to make for the Algerian coast and stop for a more thorough examination of the damage. Concerns were expressed that the ship might only make slow headway; consequently the intention was to keep to French territorial waters for as long as

76

possible then proceed independently to Malta. However, at about 22.15hrs help arrived in the form of a 'Hunt' class destroyer. This was the ubiquitous *Ledbury,* which Lieutenant Commander Hill brought alongside to enquire if the tanker needed a tow. Mason replied that engines and propeller were fine, but steering from the bridge was out and the gyrocompass not functioning. Hill said he would rig a stern light – *Ohio* should follow him on to course 120° and *'we'll . . . be in Malta for lunch'.*[16]

## Notes

[1]   *THE ITALIAN NAVY IN WORLD WAR II,* Cdr. (R) Marc' Antonio Bragadin, United States Naval Institute, 1957, p. 208.
[2]   Vic Simmons, in correspondence with the author.
[3]   Captain Mason's report to Eagle Oil, *SC88/5,* File 1, Shell Archive, Shell Centre, London.
[4]   Report of Lt. Commander Ferrini, Italian Navy Archive, Stato Maggiore della Marina, Rome.
[5]   Operational Orders and Results, Fliegerkorps II, Bundesarchiv.
[6]   Norman Smart, *Daily Express* war correspondent, aboard the cruiser *Cairo.*
[7]   While supporting the landings at Salerno in September 1943, the cruiser *Uganda* and the battleship *Warspite* were both seriously damaged by similar radio-controlled flying bombs.
[8]   Jim Perry, in correspondence with the author.
[9]   *Op.cit.* Note 3, plus report of Chief Officer Gray, same source, and PRO.ADM 199/1243, report of Lieutenant Denys Barton.
[10]  Chief Engineer James Wyld's report to Eagle Oil, *SC88/5,* File 1, Shell Archive, Shell Centre, London.
[11]  Quoted in an Australian newspaper, *The Courier-Mail,* 17 February 1992, article supplied to the author by Ray Morton.
[12]  Ray Morton, in correspondence with the author.
[13]  *Ibid.*
[14]  PRO.ADM 199/1243, Rear Admiral Burrough's report.
[15]  *DESTROYER CAPTAIN,* Roger Hill, Wm. Kimber & Co., 1975, p. 71.
[16]  *Ibid.*

# CHAPTER SIX

# THURSDAY THE 13TH

## I

Against all expectations, by midnight Chief Engineer Wyld and the engine room personnel had worked *Ohio* up to 15 knots. Yawing considerably at first, but with her rudder set 5° to starboard to counteract the effect of the splayed pump room shell plating, her course stabilised a little. Chief Officer Gray manned the wheel at the aft position where there was no wheel indicator, and from where it was not possible to see *Ledbury* just ahead. However, fortune smiled on the struggling tanker as both the helm recorder on the bridge and the telephone connection to the aft steering position were in operation, allowing Captain Mason to con the ship by passing instructions to Gray. All that night Chief Steward Francis Meeks, Second Steward John Stephens and Assistant Stewards John Church and Raymond Banner worked unceasingly to ensure that, with the crew at action stations, nobody went without food and drink. All the while furious bursts of gunfire, punctuated by fierce explosions, could be seen from the convoy ahead, now under attack from some form of surface craft.

These were ten Italian and two German torpedo boats. For the British warships, these small, highly manoeuvrable, exceptionally fast craft (35 to 40 knots), proved to be exceedingly difficult opponents at night and in the confines of the Narrows, with sea room further restricted by minefields. Radar proved ineffective at tracking them, while the escorts were reluctant to use flares as they would illuminate the convoy as much as its assailants. The Italian MS and larger MAS boats, plus the two German 'S' type attack craft lay in wait in the darkness with engines stopped until a suitable target approached, whereupon engines were gunned and in ones and twos they roared at high speed into the attack, launched torpedoes and vanished back into the night.

The torpedo boats were in their element, and at 01.08hrs had their first success. It was an important one. *MS16* and *MS22* swept in to attack *Manchester* and she was hit starboard side amidships. Two merchantmen in her wake took drastic avoiding action as she slewed to a stop, listing badly. The damage proved to be extensive, and without hope of a tow she was scuttled almost two hours later. For Rear Admiral Burrough the mounting difficulties were now in danger of spiralling out of control – should he encounter heavy units of the Italian fleet the following day, he had very little left with which to defend what might remain of the convoy.

Having moved on from *Ohio*, Burrough ordered *Ashanti* to make for the head of the convoy, now some distance away. The Rear Admiral's improvised flagship had already been narrowly missed by an aerial torpedo during the air attacks, and as she made her way south-east at speed she just avoided several mines thought to have been cut loose by minesweeping destroyers of Force X clearing a channel up ahead. To add to the general confusion, prior to his ship being torpedoed, Captain Russell of *Kenya*, also not having had word from Burrough for some time, attempted to re-establish some semblance of order by signalling all ships that he was taking command of Force X. Captain Russell's efforts only made matters worse, and to compound the problems his ship was struck shortly thereafter.

By the time *Manchester* wallowed to a halt, *Ashanti* had closed sufficiently for Burrough to see this latest disaster for himself. In company with the crippled cruiser were *Glenorchy* and *Almeria Lykes* (which must have used all her designed maximum 16 knots and more to catch up with the lead ships), while somewhat astern *Melbourne Star*, *Rochester Castle*, and *Dorset* were accompanied by the destroyer *Pathfinder*, which, however, Burrough ordered to stand by the stricken cruiser. Strung out farther astern were *Santa Elisa*, *Wairangi*, and *Waimarama*, with *Ohio*, following *Ledbury*, catching up. *Brisbane Star* made her way independently along the coastal route. Finding themselves left to their own devices, Captain Tuckett of *Dorset* and Captain Wren of *Rochester Castle* opted to attempt the alternative route around Pantelleria and down through the Sicilian Channel, and swung away to the north-east.

At 00.45hrs, *Bramham* overtook *Port Chalmers*, now just south of Zembra Island and some way astern of the other merchantmen. Shortly thereafter *Penn* joined this group and, being senior to Baines,

Lieutenant Commander J.H. Swain took them under orders. Swain reported *Port Chalmers* as being *'in some doubt as to what to do'*[1] but ordered her to follow him, and placed *Bramham* astern. Swain estimated the main body of the convoy to be between fifteen and thirty miles ahead.

Following their success against *Manchester*, the torpedo boats kept up a relentless pressure, and with the time approaching 02.00hrs, *MS31* put two torpedoes into *Glenorchy*, port side amidships, turning her into a blazing hulk which sank later that morning. At 03.00hrs, a similar fate overtook *Wairangi*, torpedoed by *MAS552* and *MAS554*. However, the Shaw Saville liner proved a difficult ship to sink. With her engines dead, Captain Gordon believed she would never reach Malta and ordered scuttling charges set and the ship abandoned. The charges failed to send her under and her Chief Engineer led a group of volunteers back aboard to finish the job. With her main cooling water pipe smashed, and watertight doors opened, she settled further but still would not go down. At daylight, the lifeboats of Gordon and his crew were still scattered forlornly around the wreck.

*Pedestal's* ordeal continued unabated. At 03.30hrs, the German boats *S30* and *S36* targeted *Almeria Lykes*, which took a hit in No.1 hold. The hold contained bagged flour, which deadened the explosion, and with her engines still fully operational the ship appears to have been in no immediate danger of sinking. Despite this, Captain Henderson ordered her abandoned, and by daylight she was still afloat. With her crew picked up by the destroyers *Somali* (Commander E.N.V. Currey, DSC) and *Eskimo* (Commander E.G. Le Geyt, DSC), Henderson suggested scuttling his ship but Currey and Le Geyt thought it better to leave her afloat in case she might yet be brought in to Malta. Vice Admiral Syfret was later scathing in his criticism of the abandonment of *Almeria Lykes*, but the American merchant marine was still new to the war, and in the European theatre had little experience of actions as relentless as this.

The second American freighter with the convoy, *Santa Elisa*, was hit not far from her compatriot by a torpedo from *MAS564*, also starboard side in No.1 hold, following a running machine-gun fight with two of the Italian boats. *Santa Elisa*, however, carried aviation spirit forward, not flour, and her forepart soon blazed fiercely. As attempts were made to bring the fire under control an explosion blew burning petrol skywards, which then dropped back onto the ship, starting a fire aft. The order to abandon ship was given, and the crew took to the boats.

Commander Swain of *Penn* elected to avoid the torpedo boats by risking the minefields south of Cape Bon, and led *Port Chalmers* and *Bramham* successfully through the area. At 04.30hrs, Oerlikon fire was seen ahead followed by an explosion, and as dawn broke the little convoy came across the burning *Santa Elisa*. Swain sent *Port Chalmers* on ahead while he and *Bramham* stopped to pick up survivors. Having completed their rescue operation, *Penn* sped after the Commodore's ship, while *Bramham* remained to finish off *Santa Elisa*. However, before the destroyer had a chance, a Ju88 swooped overhead dropping a stick of bombs on the freighter, which blew up and sank in minutes.

*Rochester Castle*, following astern of *Dorset* in attempting the northern route around Pantelleria, was spotted by Burrough in *Ashanti* and ordered back to the main body of the convoy. At around 03.29hrs, the Union Castle freighter spotted *MAS564* stopped close by off her starboard bow, and engaged the torpedo boat with machine-gun fire, scoring hits which forced the Italians to draw off. However, torpedoes were spotted shortly afterwards and *Rochester Castle* was struck starboard side in No.3 hold. The ship maintained headway at a steady 13 knots and her crew set about shoring up bulkheads. By 04.15hrs lookouts spotted ships ahead, and she had rejoined the convoy.

★   ★   ★   ★

Through the night *Ohio* followed *Ledbury*, but being initially some way astern of the main body she seems to have been missed altogether by the torpedo boats. There were a few tense moments when *Ledbury's* radar picked up a small ship off the starboard bow, but Roger Hill trained binoculars on her and saw that she was on an opposite course and towing a target. The French navy were apparently carrying out a practice shoot – *'and a hell of a night they had chosen'*. With guns trained on the vessel, Hill ordered them not to fire, *'it will give our position away – let the bastards go unless she fires or signals'*[2]. Later that night the ships also passed by the blazing wrecks of *Glenorchy*, *Wairangi* and *Almeria Lykes*. Hill would have liked to have searched for survivors but could not leave the tanker, and as he believed *Penn* to be coming up astern he pressed on.

By 06.00hrs, *Ohio* had caught up with the main body, and in view of her steering difficulties was placed at the end of a single line of merchantmen comprising *Rochester Castle*, *Waimarama* and *Melbourne*

81

*Star.* Some ten miles astern, *Port Chalmers* could be seen coming up in company with *Penn* and *Pathfinder*, and having made the hazardous journey alone around Pantelleria, *Dorset* also appeared to be well on schedule to rejoin. H.M. ships present were the cruisers *Charybdis* and the damaged *Kenya*, destroyers *Ledbury, Ashanti, Intrepid, Icarus* and *Fury*, with *Bramham* closing at 22 knots. *Somali* and *Eskimo* Burrough despatched to stand by *Manchester*, unaware that she had already sunk, then set about making the best dispositions he could for the expected arrival on the scene of major Italian surface units, plus the inevitable return of the bombers.

# II

What Admiral Burrough did not expect, however, was that the Axis High Command would leave the door to Malta, if not open, then certainly farther ajar than he could have any reason to hope.

By the morning of the 13 August, convoy and escort were critically weakened – now was the moment for the Italian cruisers to deliver the *coup de grâce*. As combined submarine and air attacks began to unravel the cohesive formation and defence of *Pedestal* around 20.00hrs on the 12th, the final element of the *Supermarina* plan, already under way, progressed well enough as Admiral Da Zara gathered his cruiser force together at a predetermined rendezvous in the Tyrrhenian Sea. His battle group comprised heavy cruisers of the 3rd Division, *Bolzano, Goriza* and *Trieste*, plus 7th Division light cruisers *Muzio Attendolo, Raimondo Montecuccoli* and *Eugenio Di Savoia*, supported by eleven destroyers, more than enough to overwhelm Burrough's scratch force. Da Zara headed south-west, his intention being to skirt the western coast of Sicily and approach Pantelleria on the morning of the 13th, perfectly placed to complete a stunning Axis victory. There remained one requirement for the final element of the plan to work: he needed air cover.

The Axis High Command were well aware that Spitfires were reinforcing Malta's fighter strength, in addition to which the island's bomber force may also have been built up. *Supermarina* needed a fighter umbrella over the battle group, but due to losses and other factors were told that *Superaero* did not have sufficient aircraft available. Fighter cover would have to come from the Luftwaffe. As Da Zara concentrated his forces in the Tyrrhenian Sea, a high level meeting, convened at the headquarters of Field Marshal Kesselring in Rome, attempted to reach agreement on the request for Luftwaffe support. As mentioned in a previous chapter, Kesselring held a low opinion of the Italian Navy and, well aware of the success that air attacks were having against the convoy, believed his fighters would be better employed supporting continued bomber assaults. German Admiral Weichold, present at the meeting to support the *Supermarina* case, later reported that *'this provoked a heated discussion among the staffs of the various services, in the course of which the representatives of the two navies found themselves alone against the other chiefs. At this point Mussolini was telephoned to give a final decision, which he made in favour of the air arm. As a result the cruiser operation, which had already gotten under way, was called off'* [3].

The pulling back of the cruisers had an unfortunate postscript for the Italian navy, as on their return to base they strayed across the path of the British submarine *Unbroken*, operating out of Malta. Her commander, Lieutenant A. Mars, placed his boat hoping for such an eventuality, but could scarcely believe his luck when six cruisers came into view. In the subsequent attack *Unbroken* put a torpedo into both *Bolzano* and *Muzio Attendolo*, damaging them to such an extent that they took no further part in the war.

★   ★   ★   ★

Given sufficient determination by the Italian cruisers, which should not have been in doubt bearing in mind their overwhelmingly superior firepower, they must surely have unleashed havoc on the convoy. Consequently withdrawing them must be considered a tactical error – one error followed in short order by another.

With Malta's reconnaissance aircraft keeping a close watch on Da Zara's cruisers, Admiral Burrough was notified as soon as it became clear that they were pulling back. This considerably eased his burden, and he benefited from another unexpected bonus when the initial Axis air attacks of the morning for some reason concentrated on the already damaged and abandoned ships previously referred to. As she overhauled the convoy, *Dorset* was in fact ignored by several aircraft, which then proceeded to use the battered hulks for target practice – and while they were thus distracted the convoy made its way mile by precious mile closer to Malta.

With the merchantmen forming line astern of *Charybdis*, the main body of the convoy – *Rochester Castle, Waimarama, Melbourne Star* and *Ohio* (with *Port Chalmers* and *Dorset* now close to rejoining this group) – endured its first air attack of the morning at 08.10hrs. Attention focused on three Italian torpedo bombers to the south, and missed a number of Ju88s flying high overhead, which then swooped on *Waimarama*. The Shaw Saville freighter took hits from three bombs and exploded in a sheet of flame. Suddenly aircraft were everywhere and the convoy found itself under severe attack. With her engines aft, *Ohio* was easily recognisable as a tanker, and selected for particular attention. Bombs fell close enough to shake the vessel severely, each near miss putting intense pressure on the tear in her hull and deck plating. Following astern of *Waimarama*, *Melbourne Star* had no time to avoid the pool of burning kerosene, fuel oil and aviation spirit that rapidly spread outwards from the doomed ship and sailed through the conflagration, narrowly missing the wreck. Gunners forward on the Blue Star Line ship quickly ran back to the midships superstructure and dodged inside as flames swept along her deck. Gunners on the aft gun positions had nowhere to run and jumped overboard.

Next in line, Captain Mason ordered *Ohio* hard aport – with kerosene tanks blown open and leaking into the sea, to go through those flames would bring an instantaneous end to her voyage. As the tanker narrowly missed the fire, a bomb burst under her forefoot, opening up her bows and filling her forepeak with water. *Ohio* shook violently from end to end, a deluge of water swamped her deck and the tear in her hull screeched in protest.

Burrough ordered *Ledbury* to stand by *Waimarama* and pick up survivors, *'although it seemed unlikely there would be any'*[4]. As mentioned, despite the fact that events surrounding PQ17 had been beyond their control, the officers and men of the destroyer believed that in some way they had failed the merchant marine during that operation. Now, however, their perceived atonement was at hand. The fire around the freighter roared hundreds of feet high and rolling smoke and flames covered a great expanse of sea. Hill later recalled that the signal from Burrough read *'Survivors, but don't go into the flames'*, and as *Ledbury* edged closer to the inferno he could not believe that anybody would be left alive. To add to his problems, Italian aircraft dropped more of the *motobomba* circling mines around the burning ship, and Ju88s swept in to attack the destroyer. Unbelievably, survivors were seen bobbing around in the water, and then waving arms and faces blackened with oil. *Ledbury* let go her whaler, with gunner Charles Musham in command, and left them to

84

pick up the more distant men. Now engaged in a desperate race against the flames, Hill took his ship in closer to what remained of *Waimarama*, landing nets were thrown over the side and crewmen leapt into the water to bring back survivors, a number of whom were badly burned. The deadly mixture of burning petrol and oil spread, and at one stage measured the length of the destroyer as she attempted to pick up two men close to the after landing nets. Hill had to go astern with the survivors supported by crewmen who were themselves clinging to the nets. As she strove to rescue as many as possible, *Ledbury* twice had to pass a man in the water who was betwixt and between destroyer and whaler, but mercifully some way from the fire. On both occasions, as she went past, Hill heard the man call out *'don't forget the diver, sir'*[5].

Finally there seemed to be no one left in the water, and Hill made ready to return to the whaler. However, the coxswain in the wheelhouse below reported a man on a raft in the flames. Through his forward-looking porthole he was able to locate the survivor who, because of the swirling smoke, had not been visible from the bridge. Hill hesitated. He could see nothing but thick smoke and flames and wondered if the ship would blow up if he took her right into the fire. The smoke then cleared for an instant and he glimpsed a man sitting on a raft of wreckage, surrounded by burning oil, with his arm raised to the destroyer. Hill took the ship in, shouting to his First Lieutenant *'for Christ's sake be quick'*. With flames higher than the mast, a roaring noise and choking smoke all around her, *Ledbury* approached her quarry. *'Jesus'*, remarked the phlegmatic Yeoman, *'it's just like a film'*[6].

The destroyer, in common with all the ships of *Pedestal*, had now been in almost continuous action for days. Unsurprisingly, fatigue began to make itself felt, and an order was repeated incorrectly. Much to Hill's regret, as he believed it may have contributed to the man's injuries, *Ledbury* had to go around for a second attempt to get to the raft. As the destroyer again ploughed through the fire, ship's cook Reginald Sida emerged from his galley aft to see what all the fuss was about. Seeing man and raft he took off his apron, kicked off his boots, and diving over the side pulled the survivor to the after landing net and helped him climb. Hill could wait no longer and as they clambered up the net called through a loud hailer *'Hold on like hell, I'm going astern'*. *Ledbury* came out of the fire in a hurry and miraculously both men were still there, Sida with one arm around the man's neck, the other through the net. They were helped aboard and the destroyer moved off to pick up Musham and the whaler. Eighty-seven crewmen from *Waimarama* lost their lives, but *Ledbury* had forty-five survivors (including several of the gunners who jumped from *Rochester Castle*). The rescue operation had taken two hours, and Hill estimated that he must by now be thirty miles astern of the convoy. Fuel had begun to assume some significance, since in the event that *Ohio* did not get through, there would be no refuelling at Malta and it was becoming touch and go whether *Ledbury* could make it to the island and back to the Fleet tanker waiting off Algiers to refuel the warships. At 09.34hrs, a signal was made to Burrough – *'thirty miles astern of convoy - interrogative rejoin or go home?'* The irrepressible Lieutenant Commander Hill then answered his own question by setting course for the convoy[7].

# III

Shortly after 09.00hrs, Beaufighters and long-range Spitfires from Malta were sighted approaching what remained of *Pedestal*. They were very welcome; however due to the ships' inability to make contact, much of their firepower would be wasted chasing Axis aircraft after they had made their bomb runs. At around 09.25hrs, the second attack of the morning developed. Ju88s were again in evidence but the main strike force comprised Ju87 Stuka dive-bombers of both the Luftwaffe and *Regia Aeronautica*. The attack was *'of a most determined nature'*[8], and *Ohio* was the primary target.

Stationed on the starboard quarter of the tanker, *Penn* put up a ferocious barrage but Stukas swarmed overhead in number and she could not take them all on. *Ohio's* own gunners worked their guns like automatons, loading and firing as the distinctive aircraft with their inverted gull-wing profile peeled off from 'ranks' above and in an effort to break up the ring of defensive fire screamed in to attack from several directions at once. Somewhat ahead, *Ashanti* also blazed away, her gunners hitting a Stuka that subsequently overflew the destroyer and slammed into the side of the tanker, a wing shattering against the after part of the bridge. Large chunks of the aircraft sprayed across her deck, and Chief Officer Gray telephoned Mason on the bridge to inform him that the tail section had dropped onto the deck just in front of him.

As the crew of *Ohio* attempted to take this in, her gunners spotted a Ju88 sweeping in from the port side forward at low level. A barrage of gunfire from the tanker and other ships nearby hit the aircraft hard.

It dropped, skimmed off the sea and slammed heavily into *Ohio*'s bows, flipping over and crashing upside down on her foredeck. The attack had been under way for half an hour and there was no sign of any let-up as a Stuka roared over the tanker at masthead height to drop two sticks of bombs, three each side. Mason reported that the subsequent explosions, all exceptionally near misses, lifted the ship *'clean out of the water'*[9]. *Ohio* shook violently and a torrent of water swamped her decks.

Severe concussion from these explosions disengaged trip gear on the fuel pump, which stopped. Steam pressure dropped away from her boilers and her engines also stopped. As *Ohio* wallowed to a halt she became a sitting target, but down in the engine room Wyld and his engineers worked like demons. With the trip gear re-engaged, steam was boosted to working pressure and within fifteen minutes the ship was once more at full throttle[10]. Under way again the tanker had nevertheless dropped astern of the convoy, but *Penn* remained in attendance and all the while the fearful din of anti-aircraft fire and bomb detonations continued unabated.

Coming up astern of *Ohio*, *Dorset* found herself caught up in the attacks and was near-missed several times; however, *Bramham* had now joined the embattled group and added her welcome firepower to the barrage. Axis aircraft attacked in three separate waves, but to the exhausted crews it seemed like one long nightmare assault. At about 10.30, a 500lb bomb exploded close astern of *Ohio* and again her fuel pump and engines stopped and pressure dropped from the boilers. Circuit breakers on both the main and auxiliary electric fuel pumps were disabled, and Wyld had the steam fuel pump started. Although the starboard condenser pump was out of commission, the port pump restarted and working pressure was again achieved in the boilers. Engines were restarted but, despite coupling the main and auxiliary condensers, achieving the necessary vacuum proved impossible, most probably due to a fracture in the condenser system. Despite superhuman efforts on the part of the engineers, the fault could not be traced. However, utilising the limited vacuum available it proved possible to turn the engines at a fitful twenty rpm, which allowed *Ohio* to struggle forward at 4 knots, dropping to 2½ knots[11].

The lighting system in the engine room, auxiliary room and stokehold failed when the bomb detonated astern, so that all work was carried forward by the light of hand-held lamps plus some emergency lighting although much of this was also out of commission. At around 11.30, a severe explosion inside the port boiler furnace put out the fires, and pressure dropped to nothing. Work continued on the starboard boiler until an explosion in that furnace similarly put out the fires. The Chief Engineer reluctantly notified Mason that the engines were dead, and there would be no restarting them this time. Approaching noon, James Wyld and his engineers left the engine room and emerged blinking into the sunlight of a bright Mediterranean summer day, and the full fury of the air attack[12].

Steam pressure not only operated the engines, it drove the steering gear. With the boilers finished, Chief Officer Gray, accompanied by the Carpenter, two Pump Men and the Boatswain, disconnected the tanker's steering gear and rigged two sets of chain differential blocks with which to move the rudder[13].

★   ★   ★   ★

As Wyld and his engineers struggled to keep Ohio's engines going, at 10.45, *Dorset* was near-missed again, blowing in the shell plating in way of No.4 hold, starting a fire and flooding the engine room. Her crew immediately abandoned ship, and according to Lieutenant Baines of *Bramham*, *'had no desire to go back to her'*[14]. Baines attempted a tow, which was in the process of being secured when a pair of Ju88s made an attack. In order to give more efficient anti-aircraft cover *Bramham* cast off, upon which Baines noticed that the freighter was considerably down by the stern. Having no ships nearby to assist him, the Lieutenant signalled Burrough that, having what he believed to be 'carte blanche', he had decided to sink her. Burrough demurred however, and Baines attempted to go alongside, pass a line and keep the flooding aft under control with the destroyer's pumps.

*Ledbury* came upon *Ohio* again around noon. *Penn* circled the tanker dropping depth charges to deter submarines, and asked *Ledbury* to attempt a tow, but before a line could be passed Hill received instructions from Vice Admiral Malta, via Burrough, to move off and search for *Manchester*, which he duly did. At 13.00hrs, *Penn* passed *Ohio* a ten inch (25.4cm) manila rope, which Douglas Gray and a support party secured to the tanker's forecastle. On attempting to pull the heavily laden vessel however, the splayed pump room shell plating again acted as a rudder and *Ohio* would only move ponderously to port, dragging the destroyer with her. Efforts to move her rudder proved fruitless, Gray even attempting to work the steering winch by hand, but to no avail. Mason advised Swain that the only way would be from alongside, or with one ship ahead and one astern to keep her straight. Lieutenant Barton reported that *'by this time everyone was feeling the strain of the last forty-eight hours, and it seemed impossible under the present conditions that any progress could be made unless some other ships could assist in the tow. It seemed that the ship was nothing more than a sitting target.'*

# IV

The Seventeenth Minesweeping Flotilla at Malta was kept busy on 12 August, making regular sweeps of the channel that the convoy would take into Grand Harbour. On the morning of the 13th, Flotilla Commander H.J. Jerome, RN, received intercepted signals outlining the mounting problems facing *Dorset* and *Ohio*, and put fleet minesweepers *Hebe* and *Rye*, plus the 1st Division of Motor Launches, on notice that they might be detached to assist.

By the afternoon of the 13th, the situation had deteriorated sufficiently for *Rye* (Lieutenant J.A. Pearson, DSC, RNR) and Motor Launches 121 and 168 to be despatched to the assistance of *Ohio*, which was, in the words of Commander Jerome, *'vital to Malta'*[15].

★    ★    ★    ★

The efforts of *Penn* to shift *Ohio* alone came to naught when the tow parted and the tanker continued to drift lazily in circles. The only assistance in sight was *Bramham*, standing by *Dorset* about three miles to westward, but Swain received notification that *Rye* and the two Motor Launches were on their way. By mid-afternoon, air attacks had slackened off and Mason suggested to Swain that advantage should be taken of the respite to temporarily disembark the tanker's personnel. With the ship dead in the water there was no point to their remaining onboard until help, and a better opportunity to organise a tow, arrived. Swain agreed and *Penn* came alongside.

*Penn* must by now have presented quite a spectacle with rescued seamen cramming every square inch of deck. Even before she took on the crew of *Ohio*, Jim Perry, late of *Empire Hope*, recalls *'a couple of hundred or more survivors . . . on the deck, some with blue dye on their faces, arms, legs etc. for burns . . . The cook was giving everyone a hard boiled egg and a slice of bread (not bad when you took the mould off), or help yourself to a ship's biscuit from a big tin on the deck, plus a handful of corned beef.'*

At some time during the frantic events that followed the torpedoing of *Ohio*, Dudley Mason burned his hands, and on boarding the destroyer took the opportunity to obtain medical attention and decent bandages. Incredibly, injuries among the crew had been comparatively light, Mason's principal concerns for them being fatigue, and the fate of Ray Morton and the other missing seamen, of whom he had no word. Once aboard *Penn*, the men of the *Ohio* had a cup of tea and a welcome rest until 18.00hrs, when *Rye* and the Motor Launches appeared. Mason called his men together and explained that with two ships it might be possible to succeed with a tow, finishing by asking for any who would be prepared to re-board and assist to step forward. The entire crew volunteered.

*Ohio* now lay at approximately 36° 00' N, 12° 59' E, a little over sixty miles from Malta.

★   ★   ★   ★

Leaving *Dorset* and *Ohio* astern, the battered remnants of Force X brought three merchantmen – *Port Chalmers*, *Melbourne Star* and *Rochester Castle* – within sight of Malta, and at 15.00hrs, ships of the Seventeenth Minesweeping Flotilla, assisted by tugs and Motor Launches, inherited escort duty and began the delicate task of shepherding the freighters along the swept channel and into Grand Harbour – to the accompaniment of a rapturous reception from the people of the long-suffering islands, thousands of whom crowded every available vantage point and cheered their 'three ships a-sailing' to the echo.

Burrough came to the conclusion that his best course of action was to take Force X back to Gibraltar immediately, leaving *Penn*, *Bramham* and *Ledbury* to complete their present assignments, and rejoin as soon as possible. As his ships sped back towards Cape Bon, Rear Admiral Burrough sent a last message to *Ohio* – *'proud to have met you'*.

★   ★   ★   ★

With his crew back aboard the crippled tanker, Mason had them throw the larger pieces of aircraft and other debris that cluttered the deck over the side, and make preparations to recommence the tow. In an attempt to counteract the drift to port, steering arms were disconnected and replaced with chain blocks port and starboard sides of the quadrant, by which it was hoped to move the rudder. *Penn* passed a line, which was secured to *Ohio*'s forecastle, and again attempted to make headway. With the going painfully slow, *Rye* passed her sweep wires to *Penn*, enabling the minesweeper to veer up to 600 yards (548m) on each to keep *Penn* steady and assist the destroyer to move the leaden bulk of the tanker.

Malta's Spitfires circled above the struggling ships and engaged Axis aircraft as they returned in strength at approaching 18.30hrs. Dogfights erupted across the evening sky, but several Ju88s got through and circled the tanker before sweeping in from astern where the defensive barrage was weakest. Again the tanker rocked and bucked to the powerful blast of near misses, until a Ju88 managed a low attacking run to drop a 500lb bomb, which penetrated the boat deck forward of the funnel, passed through the engineers' accommodation and into the stokehold between the boilers, where it exploded with a blistering roar. A number of engineers below were blown on deck, dazed but otherwise mercifully unhurt, however the blast also dislodged an engine room ventilator and other debris, which collapsed, severely injuring Bombardier Peter Brown, an army gunner manning the Bofors gun. James Wyld attempted to go below to assess the damage but was unable to see due to a choking atmosphere of powdered asbestos, blown from boiler and pipe lagging as a result of the explosion.

*Rye* reported twelve bombs falling within twenty yards (eighteen metres) of her at around 20.24hrs, covering her with spray and splinters but otherwise causing no damage. Nevertheless, due to the severity of the assault the warships were obliged to cut the tow and circle the tanker in an attempt to drive off the attackers. With her engine room flooded, Mason could plainly see that the aft part of the tanker had settled several feet deeper into the water. The tear in her tortured shell plating in way of the pump room now spread further across the deck and deeper into the bulkheads. Midships deck plating not yet torn open buckled as far as the starboard side. He knew it could not be long before she broke in two completely.

To the west of *Ohio*, three Ju88s attacked *Bramham*, while two more near-missed *Dorset*. At 19.00hrs, four more Ju88s swooped down on the freighter, setting her badly afire forward and sinking her in twenty minutes. *Bramham* closed with the *Ohio* group, being heavily attacked by a mixed force of ten Ju88s and Stukas en route, arriving at 20.30hrs, where she took station as anti-submarine screen.

With air strikes continuing unabated, Mason became concerned that *Ohio* might founder at any time and requested *ML*s 121 and 168 to come alongside and take off her crew once more. Thirty-three, including James Wyld, Douglas Gray, and many of the engineers and gunners, climbed wearily aboard *ML* 168, and in the words of Gray, *'fell asleep and woke up in Malta!'* While the exhausted crewmen slept, *ML* 168 developed a fault in one engine and returned to Grand Harbour. Had any of the tanker's crewmen been consulted, they would almost certainly have elected to remain with *Ohio*. Wyld, Gray, all of them, had dug deep in their efforts to get the tanker through and would have liked to stay with her to the end, whatever that might be.

*ML* 121 took off the remainder of the crew and subsequently transferred the injured Gunner Brown and a number of others to *Penn*, though Lieutenant Barton, Second Officer James McGilligan and others remained aboard the launch, as did Captain Mason, who fell into an exhausted sleep. On the deck of the destroyer, members of the tanker's crew watched their now deserted charge as evening deepened into night. Standing among survivors from several ships – all tired, hungry, scared – the captain of one ship was heard to murmur, *'why doesn't the old cow go down and let's all get ashore'*. Understandable perhaps, but a crewman from *Ohio* had to be restrained from throwing the officer over the side[16]. It may have been this same captain who, earlier in the day, stormed up to the bridge of the destroyer and stood toe to toe with Lieutenant Commander Swain demanding to be taken to Malta. Now! Swain evidently replied equally forcefully to the effect that *'my orders are to get* Ohio *to Malta, and that is what I intend to do. NOW GET OFF MY BRIDGE!'*[17]

With the coming of night, Swain and Lieutenant Pearson of *Rye* held a conference and decided to try again, with *Rye* towing and *Penn* astern to keep her steady. Swain sent a small party drawn from his own crew under First Lieutenant George Marten, RN, back to *Ohio* to secure the lines, where they were assisted by a detachment from *Rye* under Leading Seaman Rowland Prior. Some 250 fathoms (457m) of wire were damaged on each of *Rye*'s sweeps, and required cutting free and replacement by two 3.5" (89mm) wire hawsers to each sweep. These were then made fast to the forecastle of *Ohio* and, by 22.00hrs, with *Penn* secured astern and *Bramham* maintaining anti-submarine watch, the little convoy worked up to a steady 4 knots.

# Notes

1   PRO.ADM 199/1243, Lieutenant Commander Swain's report.
2   *DESTROYER CAPTAIN*, Roger Hill, Wm. Kimber & Co., 1975, p. 72.
3   Report of Admiral Weichold, quoted in *THE ITALIAN NAVY IN WORLD WAR II*, Commander (R) Marc' Antonio Bragadin, United States Naval Institute, 1957, p. 212.
4   PRO.ADM 199/1243, Rear Admiral Burrough's report.
5   *Op.cit.* Note 2, pp. 73/74, and PRO.ADM 199/1243, Lt. Commander Hill's report.
6   *Ibid.*
7   *Ibid.*
8   *Op.cit.* Note 4.
9   *SC88/5*, File 1, Shell Archive, Shell Centre, London, Captain Mason's report to Eagle Oil.
10  *Ibid.*, Chief Engineer Wyld's report to Eagle Oil.
11  *Ibid.*
12  *Ibid.*
13  *Ibid.*, report of Chief Officer Gray to Eagle Oil.
14  PRO.ADM 199/1243, Lieutenant Baines' report.
15  *Ibid.*, report of Commander H.J. Jerome.
16  Allan Shaw, in correspondence with the author.
17  Gary Suppiger, U.S. Navy Ensign in command of the *Santa Elisa* gun crews, interviewed for the Channel 4 documentary *CONVOY*.

CHAPTER SEVEN

# A FEW DRINKS, CHOCOLATE, AND 'KISS ME QUICK' HATS . . .

I

At 04.40hrs on 14 August, the minesweepers *Hythe* and *Hebe* plus
*ML*s 134 and 162 were despatched by Commander Jerome to the
assistance of a surprise arrival on the approach to Malta, *Brisbane
Star*. After being torpedoed on the evening of the 12th and taking to
the inshore route, the freighter, under Captain F.N. Riley, made her
way along the coast, being careful to keep inside the French territorial three-mile limit. While she remained she should be safe from
Axis forces, but if discovered by the French would have twenty-four
hours to leave or be interned, which for her crew would mean prison
camps.

Vichy authorities challenged *Brisbane Star* as she crossed the Gulf
of Hammamet early on the morning of the 13th but Riley managed,
by dint of deliberately confusing the exchange of signals and heading
further out to sea, to continue without hindrance. The Captain's next
problem soon materialised however, as a submarine could be seen just
beyond the territorial limit and keeping pace with the ship, evidently
waiting for her to make a dash for Malta. All day the two vessels played
cat-and-mouse until, towards late afternoon, a gunboat of the French
coastguard appeared and ordered Riley to halt. Again attempting to
stall for time by deliberately misunderstanding the signals, Riley sailed
on until the French put a shot across his bows and he had no choice

94

but to comply. Having inspected the torpedo damage, two French officials came aboard and declared the ship unseaworthy, but Riley managed to talk them out of any notion of interning his ship and they allowed him to proceed, taking with them a wounded crewman for medical attention when they left.

At around this time, there seems to have developed among the crew a feeling that between the submarine and the French their prospects for reaching Malta were slim to non-existent, and therefore the ship should be scuttled and they would take their chances in prison camp. In his report, Captain Riley spoke of delegations sent to him with the men's demands, but Danny O'Mara, at the time an eighteen-year-old galley boy aboard *Brisbane Star*, recalls, *'there was no delegation, the crew assembled on deck with a spokesman to request that the ship be scuttled and we should be interned'*[1]. Versions of what happened next are many and varied – the naval liaison officer threatened to order the ship's gunners to open fire on the crew; a signal received confirmed that Beaufighters from Malta would provide air cover from daylight the following day; careful reconsideration was made of the unpleasant reputation that the Vichy French authorities had acquired for their treatment of British prisoners, etc. etc. For some, all, or none of these reasons the crew elected to continue, and despite his ship being considerably down by the head as a result of the torpedo hole in her bows, with the coming of dusk Captain Riley decided to try to lose the submarine among the shoals and sandbars along the coast. Finally having succeeded, *Brisbane Star* set course into the night for Malta and a rendezvous with the MLs and minesweepers at 08.20hrs on the 14th.

★    ★    ★    ★

On the afternoon of 13 August, with *Dorset* and *Ohio* under the watchful eyes of *Bramham* and *Penn* respectively, and still unaware that *Manchester* had sunk, Roger Hill had *Ledbury* come about and make for the Gulf of Hammamet in the hope that he might obtain fuel from the cruiser. At 13.45hrs, *Ledbury* circled *Waimarama*, but with no sign of life on or around the wreck the destroyer pressed on. Hill stood the ship down to two watches, allowing his crew to bathe, eat and sleep, and having visited the survivors, some of whom were badly burned, retired to his sea cabin below the bridge to grab a nap himself[2].

At approaching 15.45hrs, Hill was rudely awakened by the aircraft

95

alarm to find his ship on the point of being attacked by two triple-engined Italian bombers, both of which the Oerlikon and pom-pom crews shot down in the ensuing engagement. Hill ordered "Splice the Mainbrace" and wrote in his report, *'this success came at a very apt time as the ship's company were showing signs of very great fatigue, and the survivors were, most understandably, jumpy'*[3].

Having spent the afternoon searching along the coast without success, with the coming of night *Ledbury* retraced her route. Well before daylight, all hands were back at action stations as Hill made for the estimated position that *Ohio* should have reached. However, as black night gave way to the first rays of dawn, anti-aircraft fire split the skyline astern, and he realised they had overshot her. Coming about again, the destroyer sped for the sound of the guns.

## II

*Ledbury* was a welcome sight as she joined the little group. To those attempting to shift the tanker, a return to mere exhaustion would constitute a welcome improvement for progress during the night had been tortuously slow. Captain Mason and his crew had now been struggling with their charge for thirty hours or more, at action stations for longer than that, and with fleeting opportunities at best for sleep or rest, while the ship struggled forward under almost continuous attack. Likewise the officers and men of *Penn*, *Bramham* and *Ledbury* had all been at a high state of alert and in action for days, with little respite. Stress and fatigue will play tricks with the mind, shorten tempers and blow otherwise minor problems out of all proportion until the most routine task can adopt the proportions of a climb up the north face of the Eiger. All these effects and more each man must have endured, and yet there was no mention of abandoning or sinking *Ohio*. Discipline held, and efforts – increasingly obstinate, bloody-minded, refuse-to-be-beaten efforts – to get *Ohio* to Malta continued without let up.

At 02.30, perhaps due to *Rye* attempting a moderate increase in speed, the tanker again sheered violently to port and the tow parted. Previously, at 01.15, *Bramham* had closed with *Penn* and Lieutenant Baines suggested 6 to 7 knots might be possible with a destroyer secured either side of the crippled merchantman, rather than ahead and astern. Lieutenant Commander Swain now decided to give it a

96

try, and *Bramham* secured to the tanker's starboard side. *Penn* secured to port, but in the dark the extent to which shell plating splayed out from the damaged pump room could not be ascertained, and fearing serious damage to the warship's hull, Swain opted to cast off and wait for daylight. *Bramham* did likewise. Once again *Ohio* lay dead in the water – a tantalising twenty miles from Malta. No distance at all.

★   ★   ★   ★

Dudley Mason advised Swain that he would re-board the tanker at first light, at which time – winches and equipment aboard *Ohio* being unfamiliar to Royal Navy personnel – additional help was also called for among the numerous merchant seamen present. Many volunteered, and while a complete list is practically impossible to compile, they include Junior Third Officer Frederick A. Larsen Jr., Cadet Midshipman Francis A. Dales, British Army gunner Bill Hendy, and the Boatswain, all from *Santa Elisa;* Captain Ramsey Brown, ship's carpenter Norman Warden Owen, and five shipmates from *Deucalion;* the Boatswain from *Waimarama* (a particularly courageous act bearing in mind what he must have been through already); a contingent from *Melbourne Star;* and from *Ohio* herself, Second Officer Hector McGilligan, Chief Steward Francis Meeks, Allan Shaw, two firemen, two greasers, storekeeper Thomas Leach, the ship's radio officers, two apprentices, and several others. Roger Hill also put aboard a detachment of ratings from *Ledbury,* under Gunner Musham.

Larsen and the *Santa Elisa* survivors made for the Bofors gun on the poop deck abaft the funnel, which they found to be virtually undamaged. Assisted by three British gunners they soon had it operational, Larsen taking the trainer's position with Dales and a British gunner alternating as pointers. Musham's first act aboard was to instruct his party to check and try out all the remaining guns and it was as well that he did, for every one would be needed before the day was out. Throughout the many attacks *Ohio*'s radio officers, First Officer Alan Collins and Second Officer Dennis Smith, together with apprentices Robert Wilkinson and Henry Bulmer, had assisted the gunners at the mid-ship Oerlikons either side of the bridge. They now returned to handle the guns themselves.

With the glow of another fine summer day spilling over the eastern horizon, a further air attack swept across the little convoy. Tanker, destroyers and minesweeper all put up a spirited defence, and as air activity temporarily died away, the next attempt to get *Ohio* moving developed. *Penn* secured alongside while *Rye* stationed herself ahead to assist with the tow and keep the tanker on a steady course. A ten inch (254mm) manila rope (unearthed in the tanker's stores, fortunately well stocked by Texaco before she left the United States), secured to a wire from the forecastle of *Ohio* led around *Rye*'s sweep winch to a cable secured from *Penn* to the tanker. In this fashion the strange procession crept forward for around half an hour until the wire in the tanker's fairlead parted, and both warships cut themselves free.

Hill then suggested to Swain (senior officer present), that *Rye* and *Ledbury* should 'have a crack' at a tow, and Swain agreed. With the time at just after 07.00hrs, *Rye* stationed herself ahead of *Ohio*, passed 300 fathoms (349m) of wire from each sweep to the tanker's forecastle and took up the tow. Meanwhile, a line secured from the tanker's stern led to *Ledbury's* mid-ship bollards, the destroyer intending to act as a drag and keep the merchantman straight. At a painfully slow two knots the little procession got under way until *Ledbury* dragged a little too much, and once more the tow from *Rye* parted.

Hill tried again, having a ten inch (254mm) manila rope secured from the forecastle of the tanker to his anchor cable, which had been run aft. A tug tows from the pivotal point just abaft the funnel and can turn as she tows; a destroyer, however, has to tow from right aft, and if the tow is very heavy direction falls away and is impossible to maintain[4]. To counter this, Hill had *Rye* take a line from the destroyer's forecastle to keep her bows up, and again the two ships strained to move *Ohio*, which, true to form, sheered away to port as soon as she got underway, dragging the warships around with her. To counter this, Swain brought *Penn* in and lashed her to the tanker's starboard side and in this fashion attempted to keep her straight. This appeared to work and with the time now around 08.00hrs, the ungainly group once more set off for Malta.

As if to mock the apparent success of this attempt, the *Regia Aeronautica* sent in nine Ju87 Stukas to finish the job once and for all. As the dive-bombers peeled off overhead and screamed in to the attack, pandemonium broke loose and a furious barrage erupted from the convoy. However, with four ships lashed together and only *Bramham* able to manoeuvre, they presented a prime target. Yet again *Ohio* was near-missed, her fractured mid-ship deck plating screeching in protest as the aft end of the ship attempted to tear itself free. It seemed to Hill that a Stuka dived directly at his bridge, releasing a 500lb bomb that plummeted towards him. The aircraft roared over

98

an almost stationary *Ledbury* at masthead height, the bomb missing her forecastle by a whisker. A gout of water erupted, cascaded across the ship and everybody froze, waiting for the explosion that would blow her bows off. After a tense few seconds, a lookout noticed a spreading pool of oil alongside, and realisation dawned that the Stukas were dropping oil bombs, trying to set the tanker alight – *'we were saved by Axis thoroughness'* commented Hill[5]. With one aircraft downed by gunners aboard *Ohio*, Spitfires from Malta arrived and chased off the remainder.

Such was the intensity of the attack that attention drew away from the task at hand and *Rye*, ahead of *Ledbury*, far from keeping the destroyer on course, began a drift to starboard that dragged *Ledbury* with her. By the time the Stukas had been driven off there were four ships stopped in a row: *Ohio* with *Penn* alongside pointing approximately toward Malta, *Ledbury* alongside *Penn* but pointing the wrong way; and lastly *Rye*, also pointing the wrong way. Roger Hill later recalled that the *'chaos of wires, ropes and cables hanging down into the sea had to be seen to be believed'*[6].

From the afternoon of the 13th, Commander Jerome had been at sea in the minesweeper *Speedy*, attending first to the arrival of the three freighters and subsequently organising the arrival of *Brisbane Star*. With these tasks completed he set off for *Ohio* in company with *ML*s 135 and 459. Jerome located the group at approximately 08.30hrs, as the three warships disentangled themselves from their jumbled towing gear and by virtue of being senior officer present, took command of the operation.

★   ★   ★   ★

Having reboarded *Ohio* early that morning, Allan Shaw found himself gunner at one of her Oerlikons. In common with most British Merchant seamen, he had received instruction in firing the weapons likely to be found aboard ship in preparation for just such an eventuality as this. As the air attacks swept in he recalls *'hell knows if we ever hit anything, thousands of tracer fired . . . it was impossible to say who hit what, but you do things automatically, and it helps keep you going'*. For the now gunner Shaw, the most frustrating part of the task was locating a target and following it round, only to have the barrel hit one of the guides around the gun position. The breech then had to be depressed to lift the barrel over the guide and come down on the other side before picking up the target again. The guides were a necessary evil, designed to stop gunners shooting up their own funnel, masts, wheelhouse, etc. – all too easy to do in the heat of the moment. For Captain Ramsey Brown and the *Deucalion* contingent, initially sent below to try to find a way to improve buoyancy aft, urgent work awaited them on deck, handling winches and lines as tow after tow broke. Norman Warden Owen later recalled that *'Captain Brown worked like a galley slave, and gave us a magnificent example. We shall remember him proudly as one of the bravest men who ever trod a deck'*[7].

With several hundred survivors to feed, shortage of food had begun to be a problem, consequently Captain Mason authorised the opening of *Ohio*'s bonded stores. Seamen gleefully disappeared below to see what they could find, returning with cigarettes, *'tins of biscuits, bottles of pop, and some other liquid refreshment: Rum . . . Paddy, an Irish AB, the worse for having too much rum, wanted somebody to throw him overboard, because he was drunk. I told him I was too tired, and he managed an hour's sleep and woke up raring to go. I envied him the sleep'*[8]. Gunner Bill Hendy recalled the men below enjoying chocolate and a few drinks and getting hold of a consignment of party hats in store, awaiting a holiday of one sort or another. Gunners aboard the tanker and nearby destroyers were soon stylishly sporting an American version of the *'Kiss Me Quick'* hat – no doubt to the bafflement of any Axis pilots who may have noticed![9] Whether as the result of feeling the warm glow of a tot of rum is not known, but it was around this time that Lieutenant Commander Swain decided that everybody needed cheering up, and ordered music played over *Penn*'s PA system. Unfortunately the ship had but one record – Glen Miller's *Chatanooga Choo Choo* coupled with *Elmer's Tune*, but these were dutifully played and replayed as loud as possible, come hell, high water, or air attack.

★   ★   ★   ★

In what might be judged another error, the Axis High Command took the decision to concentrate air attacks on the morning of 14 August against Force X as it made its way back towards Gibraltar. This gave the *Ohio* group breathing space between air assaults to inch (it must have seemed almost literally to those involved) the tanker closer to Grand Harbour. Commander Jerome was not one to tinker with a good idea when he saw it, and as two ships towing with one lashed to the side appeared to be working, *Rye* to *Ledbury* to *Ohio*, with *Penn* lashed to starboard was again the order of business and once more progress was made, albeit at a 5 knot crawl.

A motor launch astern of *Ohio* reported that the aft section of the tanker appeared to be settling considerably, and the constant creaking and grinding of the mid-ships deck plating and bulkheads was ominous. Captain Mason took the opportunity offered by the lull in air activity to make an inspection of the ship, and as most of his own engineers were back in Malta, requested the assistance of the Chief Engineer and Chief Officer of *Penn* plus the loan of compressor gear as the tanker's own compressors were smashed beyond repair. Given the pounding that *Ohio* had taken, Mason might be forgiven a raised eyebrow in surprise at finding that her empty tanks were still dry and intact, which would greatly assist restoring some element of buoyancy by transferring cargo between tanks using the compressed air lines. Kerosene still overflowed from the port side wing tanks, but with the lids buckled nothing could be done with those. Mason reported to Jerome that he felt she would last another twelve hours provided she did not break in half. Mason also estimated that in the event that she did break up and, as seemed certain, the aft section sank, the forepart (containing 75 per cent of her cargo) should remain afloat and would be easier to tow.

Captain Mason also had a solemn duty to perform aboard *Penn* and boarded the destroyer to lead a service for Bombardier Brown, who had died the previous night and was duly buried at sea.

At approaching 10.50hrs, the respite was brought to a shattering end as once more Stukas of the *Regia Aeronautica*, supported by Macchi 202 fighters, screamed out of the sky. Yet again a furious barrage went up from the little group of ships and the all too familiar 'cotton wool' puffs of smoke from anti-aircraft fire quickly speckled the clear blue sky. Spitfires giving cover overhead swept down in an attempt to keep the Stukas away from the ships, and dogfights erupted as the Macchis tried equally forcefully to keep the British fighters at bay. A bomb exploded astern of *Rye*, inevitably parting the tow, while *Ledbury* and *Penn* cut themselves free of the tanker, the better to manoeuvre and offer effective covering fire. In the mêlée above, a Stuka broke free from the dogfights to dive in at *Ohio*, dropping a 1,000lb (454kg) bomb which exploded immediately astern, the terrific concussion throwing the ship forward, tearing off her rudder and blowing a huge hole in her after peak tank. This must surely be the end as steel plates in the mid-ships section ground together, twisted and buckled – but once again this extraordinary ship held together. However, as the Stukas were driven off, it was self evident that she could not take much more.

# III

Commander Jerome wasted no time in getting another tow organised, ordering *Bramham* in to the port side of the tanker, *Penn* to starboard, while *Rye* again took station ahead. Towlines were fixed, hawsers in place, and once again *Ohio* moved desperately slowly towards Grand Harbour. Unsurprisingly, the engine room of the tanker now flooded at an even greater rate, and the destroyers' pumps worked flat out in an attempt to keep the level down. Still the water gained at a rate of 6 inches (152mm) per hour; freeboard aft was down to 2 feet 6 inches (0.76m), and Mason expected the aft section to break away momentarily.

At 12.27, the hawsers to *Bramham* parted and progress stopped as drained minds aboard tanker and destroyer attempted to instruct hands, which by now felt full of thumbs, to reconnect towlines. With *Bramham* again securely alongside, Jerome ordered that *Rye* should cast off and the attempt be made with just the two destroyers lashed to the tanker's sides. A steady 5 knots again materialised and was maintained until 19.28hrs, when, heartbreakingly, the lines parted again.

As bone-weary seamen from the destroyers and from *Deucalion,* and *Santa Elisa, Melbourne Star* and *Waimarama,* from *Ohio* herself, and doubtless other men from other ships whose names have gone unrecorded, moved like zombies to fix the lines, at last a sight to breathe new life into flagging spirits hove in view in the unlikely shape of the converted trawlers *Beryl* and *Swona,* plus the ancient (built 1907) steam paddle tug *Robust.* It was not that much help was expected from these additions to the little armada, but if they could make it from Grand Harbour to this solitary patch of ocean, then surely to God *Ohio* must by now be close to Malta.

Commander Jerome ordered *Robust* to secure a line to the tanker's forecastle to assist the destroyers with the tow. This having been arranged the little group once more set out, but *Ohio* had not mended her ways and broke away to port, her forefoot sliding over the tow from the tug before the destroyers or *Robust* could counter the movement. *Robust* swung round on the end of the line, by now too taut to be

102

slipped, and struck *Penn* with her stern, holing the destroyer above the waterline in way of the wardroom and after cabin flat. The air around Lieutenant Commander Swain evidently turned blue for some little while thereafter. *Robust* damaged her stern and rudder and Jerome ordered her back to Malta. With dusk now deepening into night, further air attacks were expected but did not materialise, and Roger Hill probably expressed the feelings of all concerned when he later recalled *'I felt if we had any more bombs around I would lie down on the deck and burst into tears . . . '*[10].

With *Ohio* once more in the care of *Penn* and *Bramham*, the convoy crawled forward again, and as the last vestiges of daylight on 14 August receded from the sky, the southern cliffs of Malta were sighted.

The dim outline in the distance brought cheers of exultation from the exhausted crews, but they were not home yet. The desperately unwieldy tanker had still to be nursed through the narrow swept channel between minefields around the entrance to Grand Harbour, and at any time attacks from submarines or torpedo boats might still develop. At approaching midnight, *Ohio* entered the swept channel and Commander Jerome rearranged the accompanying minesweepers and launches to form an anti-submarine and torpedo-boat screen to seaward. The journey at snail's pace through the channel in pitch dark proved perilous in the extreme, and more than once *Ohio* attempted to slew away to port. At these moments, activity aboard the destroyers lashed to her sides would be frenetic with Lieutenants Baines and Swain shouting across *Ohio* to each other, coordinating their efforts, altering engine revolutions – one ship push, one pull – slowly, delicately, drag her away from the mines, make sure she doesn't swing too far the other way . . .

At these moments, *Ledbury* acted as a mobile rudder, gingerly pushing the tanker this way and that with her bows to bring her back on course. Two major changes of direction would be needed: the first north-west for the run up to Valetta, the second a 140° swing to port for the entrance to Grand Harbour. As the first of these changes took place, Malta's coastal defences opened fire, erroneously believing they had sighted torpedo boats. Gunfire into the minefields with a loaded tanker in the vicinity was a nightmare that nobody needed and the destroyers frantically switched on recognition lights, flashed signals, and fired coloured lights for night-time recognition until finally the gunfire subsided.

By 03.00hrs on the morning of the 15th, the ancient battlements of Valetta were just discernible as darker shapes against the night sky, port side abeam the slow moving group. *Ledbury* moved into position alongside the tanker and with the assistance of an ML pushing the bow of the destroyer, swung *Ohio* round in three hauls, turning her approximately 45° each time. With the tanker gently moving ahead once more, Grand Harbour came into view as the final dawn of this epic voyage brightened into morning. At 05.00hrs, Assistant King's Harbour Master J.P. Pilditch arrived aboard the small steam tank vessel *Supply,* accompanied by the tugs *Carbine* and *Lady Strickland. Supply* berthed alongside *Penn* while Pilditch boarded the destroyer accompanied by the Senior Pilot; and it would hardly be surprising if it were not with some relief that Commander Jerome handed charge of the tow into Grand Harbour over to the Assistant King's Harbour Master. Pilditch had *Carbine* pass a wire to the stern of *Ohio* and with the tug steering and destroyers lashed either side, she approached the boom at the harbour entrance.

As with the freighters the day before, *Ohio* received a tumultuous reception from the Maltese, who again crammed every available space in order to catch a glimpse of the battle-scarred veteran. Tired as they were, the crews, merchant and naval alike, were deeply moved by the emotional intensity of their welcome from a people who had endured extremes of danger and privation for many long months.

With water continuing to gain ground in the tanker's engine room, freeboard aft was such that a man lying on deck might trail his hand in the sea. As she passed through the boom, *Ohio* once more dragged her companions off course, this time to starboard, obliging *Lady Strickland* to pass a line to the recalcitrant merchantman's bows to bring her round. *Robust* replaced *Penn* alongside, and finally the tanker allowed herself to be nudged gently into Bighi Bay. At 09.30 she berthed alongside the tanker *Plumleaf* at Parlatorio Wharf, and her long ordeal was over. Again Roger Hill probably encapsulated the thoughts of many – *'It was Saturday morning; years and years ago we had left Gibraltar and that was last Sunday morning. It did not make sense, but all this had only taken a week'*[11].

## Notes

1    Danny O'Mara, in correspondence with the author.
2    *DESTROYER CAPTAIN*, Roger Hill, Wm. Kimber & Co., 1975, p. 75.
3    PRO.ADM 199/1243, Lieutenant Commander Hill's report.
4    *Op.cit.,* note 2 p. 79.
5    *Ibid.,* p. 82.

6    *Ibid.*, p. 82.
7    Scrapbook of Norman Warden Owen, as supplied to the author.
8    Allan Shaw, in correspondence with the author. Allan also recalls meeting 'Paddy' again in 1943, in the Fleet Club in Taranto. The pair of them won *'a carrier bag full of lira'* on the lotto, and celebrated in suitably liquid fashion.
9    Bill Hendy, interviewed for the Channel 4 documentary, *CONVOY*.
10   *Op.cit.*, note 2, p. 84.
11   *Ibid.*, p. 85.

## CHAPTER EIGHT

# WHEN THE HURLYBURLY'S DONE . . .

## I

The job finally completed, Dudley Mason handed *Ohio* over to representatives of the Naval Fuelling Authority, who arranged for the discharge of cargo to commence immediately. He also gave instructions for all ship's fittings, stores, and everything movable and/or salvable to be taken ashore and stored, as the ship might founder at any moment. The unshaven, sweat-streaked melange, the happy band of brothers who now comprised his crew, Mason said should collect gear if they had it and proceed ashore where digs would be found for them.

Allan Shaw struggled aft to his cabin, clambering over wires, towlines, wreckage, and pipelines, finally arriving to find *'my locker door open, all gear covered in asbestos shaken from the bulkheads, which were fireproofed'*. Allan rescued his mate Ken Arundel's gear from his still shut locker and took a last look around, including a trip to the bridge where he salvaged a pair of Navy binoculars that he later returned to Lieutenant Barton who he found lodged at the Meadowbank Hotel, Sliema, along with a number of *Ohio* veterans. Many of the merchant seamen remained in Malta for a month or more, a few attempting to stow away aboard ships bound for the UK. but without success. Finally Allan Shaw and Ken Arundel were put aboard a Hudson bomber and flown to Gibraltar where, after one day, they were able to hitch a lift aboard the Australian destroyer *Quiberon*, calling at The Rock to refuel while escorting a damaged

106

Dutch cruiser from the Far East to the Clyde for repairs. *Quiberon* was evidently a happy ship, with what the Aussies described as '*a mad English Skipper*' and what Allan Shaw describes as '*a grand crew who wouldn't let us pay for anything in the NAAFI canteen. They treated us well.*'

Once on the quay in Grand Harbour, Jim Perry and the rest of the survivors were told to stay in groups and await transport. Spying a shipmate from a previous voyage, the two got together and were taken with a group of others to a huge cave close by, given a tot of rum and a plate of stew and told to await transport. Noticing *Port Chalmers* docked nearby, Jim's mate suggested they go aboard for a beer as he knew the Second Steward. Sitting with their feet up aboard ship having a quiet drink with the Second in the crew's messroom, the door swung open and in walked another flustered steward to ask what the bloody hell they were doing there! It transpired that Jim knew the new arrival and explained that he had been shipwrecked. '*Lucky bastard*', replied the steward, '*I'm run off my feet with all the people coming onboard for meals!*'

Dudley Mason also took time for a last look over his battered command and came to the after wheel position, manned for as long as it remained operational by Chief Officer Douglas Gray. With no shelter or protection Gray steered the ship all through the night of the 12th and into the ferocious air attacks of the 13th, the deck around the wheel now strewn with debris, splinters, machine-gun bullets and cartridge cases, bearing silent witness to the Chief Officer's exceptional courage. Gray was also destined for a lively journey home. Despatched to Gibraltar he took command (his first) of an 'old tub' called the *Omega* with orders to take her back to the U.K. Crossing the Bay of Biscay, the ship encountered very heavy weather, and subsequently came under attack from a long range Focke Wulf Fw 200 Condor bomber – which the ship's gunners shot down![1]

Galley boy Danny O'Mara stayed aboard *Brisbane Star* as she was patched up and returned to service. After surviving *Pedestal* and months in Malta under what seemed like constant air attack, the ship made a dash for Suez then down the East African coast to Mombasa and The Cape. With the ship 'double parked' in Cape Town, the ship's cook, Danny's immediate boss, decided to make a trip ashore alone one night, requiring the negotiation of a narrow plank between *Brisbane Star* and the freighter alongside in order to get to the wharf. The cook's body was found next morning, washing against the ship's side. It seemed to Danny that having survived so much, this was an ironic way for a life to end, and he has been a firm believer in fate ever since.

*Brisbane Star* did not return to the U.K. until April 1943. As a result of events surrounding the 'scuttling' incident, on arrival the crew were kept onboard for two days while the ship was searched and any material relating to *Pedestal* confiscated. Each crewmember then found himself obliged to sign the Official Secrets Act before signing off the ship. A junior engineer named Parlour, caught attempting to smuggle ashore his personal diary of the action, was tried, convicted, and sentenced to ten years imprisonment. Sixty years after the event, Danny O'Mara is still subject to the provisions of the OSA.

★   ★   ★   ★

Although he didn't know it until later, when Ray Morton was blown over the side on the 12<sup>th</sup> he was judged to have left the ship and his pay stopped from the moment he hit the drink! This was standard practice during the war years and also applied to merchant seamen whose ships were sunk. From the moment they took to the boats, pay stopped. Something else Ray discovered the hard way – if a seaman spent four weeks or more getting home (as he did) or in a lifeboat or life raft, that was his month's survivor's leave used up.

Having spent time recuperating aboard *Bicester* as she escorted the damaged *Manchester*, Ray and Mario Guidotti were landed at Gibraltar. A first priority was to get some money, but the only advice available to the two survivors was to 'get a job!' This proved to be easier said than done, and killing time one day walking along the dock *'a guy in bell bottoms'* approached Ray and asked if he were Jack Morton's lad. *'Yeah'*, he replied, puzzled. *'Have a beer with your old man in the Crown and Thistle on Saturday afternoons when I'm home'*, said the stranger and strolled off with that rolling walk that seamen have ashore, as though they still have the heaving deck of a ship beneath their feet. Both Ray and Mario managed to obtain labouring jobs in the navy shipyards, but were repatriated to the U.K. aboard the Union Castle passenger/cargo vessel *Llanstephan Castle* before being able to collect their first pay packet.

Ray thought no more of the dockside incident, but at home his parents received the standard telegram: *'Regret to inform you your son is missing at sea and must be pronounced killed by enemy action'*. On Sunday 16 August, Ray's parents tuned in to the nine o'clock BBC radio news to hear an Admiral of the Fleet describe in glowing terms the story of Operation *Pedestal*, which did little to reassure them beyond convincing them that their dead son was now a dead hero. The following day better news arrived with a second telegram: *'Following last night's broadcast can now advise you your son is safe and alive. Under no circumstances should you attempt to contact him.'* This last sentence raised more questions than it answered. What had happened? Was he injured? Was he crippled? Some days later their prayers were answered in the form of a letter from Mr Morton Senior's drinking mate in Gibraltar, advising them that, aside from being somewhat the worse for wear on navy rum, their son was in tolerably good condition.

Ray Morton has one more story to tell of that voyage, concerning his Bible, which it may be remembered he left in his cabin aboard ship. Having spent a month or more in Gibraltar, Ray finally arrived home and a few days thereafter received a visit from the local vicar. To Ray's complete amazement, the vicar had come to return his Bible, inside which was a letter from the finder to the Bible and Tract Society asking them to pass the book along to the vicar and for him to return it to the 'bereaved' parents. The letter, written by Able Seaman C.F. Cliffe of Wairarapa, New Zealand, was dated Avonmouth 21 September 1942, and explained that after his ship had been sunk during *Pedestal*, he had been picked up by a destroyer and subsequently boarded *Ohio* to help out with the tow. Late one afternoon, following her arrival in Malta, Cliffe and one or two others went back aboard the tanker to search among the debris for anything that might be useful – *'odds and ends, such as a piece of soap to wash with or an old pair of trousers to replace our dirty ones, which we had damaged during rescue work . . . '*

In the wrecked accommodation, Cliffe came across the Bible in what had been Ray Morton's cabin. Having lost his own copy, the seaman kept it until such time as he could purchase another, and then returned it. Ray tried everything he could think of to contact Able Seaman Cliffe to thank him, but without success. He still has the Bible and the letter, and makes sure they go with him whenever he moves.

# II

With the thunderous welcome from the Maltese as a backdrop – bands playing, people cheering – Roger Hill described watching *Ohio* being pushed into position to discharge her invaluable cargo as the most wonderful moment of his life. He then made a quick tour of his ship, *'got some dope from Doc'*, retired to his cabin and fell into an exhausted sleep[2].

Awaking the following day, Hill found an invitation to lunch with Lord Gort at Antonio Palace awaiting his attention. Despite the arrival of five *Pedestal* ships, things were still spartan in Malta, and the meal comprised a vegetable omelette. During their conversation, Gort confided that if *Pedestal* had been a complete failure, as had so many previous attempts, he would have had to surrender the island within sixteen days. With the meal completed the two men shook hands, and Gort rode off on his bicycle.

On 18 August, *Ledbury* sailed for Gibraltar in company with *Penn* and *Bramham*. Leaving Malta to return across that thousand miles of ocean, so recently the stage for events he thought he might never survive, Hill suffered a violent reaction. With knees shaking, feeling sick and terrified, he discreetly retired to his cabin as soon as he was able, there to be violently sick[3].

By the time the trio of destroyers reached Gibraltar, Hill had recovered his composure enough to suggest to Swain and Baines that they should put in a claim for salvage of the *Ohio*. Swain declined, but Baines and Hill duly wrote to the Admiralty. Wheels within the Civil Service move exceeding slow, particularly when it comes to paying out money, and it was not until two and a half years had passed that Hill received his share as captain of one of the three ships involved – £19 18s 4d[4]. Slow they may have been, but everybody aboard the RN ships got their share. Lieutenant Keith Frost, then a gunner aboard *Ledbury*, recalls receiving a cheque for £2 19s 4d as his proportion of the salvage money[5].

Incredibly, and despite continuing to be in the thick of the action, Roger Hill received no further promotion and finished the war a Lieutenant Commander. On his death in 2001, Lieutenant Commander Hill's ashes were fittingly scattered in the Mediterranean off Malta, the island that he and *Pedestal* had done so much to save.

Eagle Oil seems to have been a happy company, a good employer, and a fairly run company for its entire staff. However, even in the best-run operations, the dead hand of the narrow-minded accountant can be felt, and there was apparently a suggestion abroad that pay for the crew of *Ohio* should stop from the time the ship was 'abandoned' on 13 August. Dudley Mason, however, felt the crew to be entitled to Shipwreck Indemnity pay as they only left due to the severity of the bombing, and with the ship dead in the water. Mason pointed out that all volunteered to reboard when the time came and that none of the crew abandoned ship of their own volition, despite the fact that for the final two days of the voyage their quarters were uninhabitable. Eagle Oil subsequently agreed that pay should continue up to 15 August, with the exception, as mentioned, of the four crewmen who were blown over the side on the 12th [6].

★　　★　　★　　★

Norman Warden Owen, the carpenter from *Deucalion*, received the DSM for his efforts aboard *Ohio*. He also got a hero's welcome on returning to his native Wales, although he was (and still is) reluctant to expand on his role in getting *Ohio* through, believing '*I only did my work*'. In 1951, while working as a diver for British Railways, Norman made a dive off the Old Mall Pier, Holyhead. Twenty-seven feet below the surface, while fitting a block and tackle to haul the stump of an old pile from the seabed, the two middle fingers of his right hand became trapped when the block slipped. With the hand trapped he had no means of controlling the air valve on his helmet and no way to contact the other members of the three-man team on the pier. Well aware that he could not remain where he was for any length of time, Norman cut off the fingers with his sheath knife. Finally back on dry land, his workmates removed the helmet to be calmly told to '*keep cool, don't hurry*'. He then walked to the local hospital for medical attention. Norman received the Order of Industrial Heroism for his courage, awarded by the *Daily Herald*, a popular national daily newspaper of the time.

Norman Warden Owen evidently has salt water in his veins as, well into his eighties, he still races yachts competitively. He also passed his love of the sea on to his two sons, one of whom is Master of an ocean-going cruise liner, the other coaching a team bidding for the America's Cup.

★　　★　　★　　★

On 22 May 1943, United States National Maritime Day, before 2,300 cadet-midshipmen assembled at the newly constructed O'Hara Hall at the United States Merchant Marine Academy, Junior Third Officer Frederick A. Larsen Jr. and Cadet Midshipman Francis A. Dales received from Deputy Administrator Captain Edward

Macaulay, USN (Ret.), the Merchant Marine Distinguished Service Medal, in recognition of their efforts during the *Pedestal* convoy, firstly aboard *Santa Elisa,* and after she was sunk, in volunteering to man the Bofors gun aboard *Ohio.* Francis Dales was only the third Cadet Midshipman to receive the award. His basic training began at Fort Schuyler in February 1942, completed at King's Point, and he shipped out for his first voyage in late April[7], a mere four months prior to *Pedestal.*

★    ★    ★    ★

Because of the burns to his hands, it was decided that Dudley Mason should be flown home for treatment, and following a few days in Malta he boarded a Douglas DC3 'Dakota' in company with James Wyld. The two seamen must have presented a rare spectacle, having lost all their belongings and been supplied with any clothes that came to hand – all odds and ends, none of which fitted. The aircraft had been stripped out and the two men were obliged to sit on mailbags for the flight home, their only companions being a few civilians from a Ministry of one sort or another.

The flight had been under way for several hours when Mason looked out of a window and called over to Wyld, *'just look where we are'.* One of the 'Men from The Ministry' immediately blew his top – the flight was secret he fulminated – they had no business knowing where they were! As patiently as he was able, Mason explained that they were flying over the North Devon coast, his parents home was practically below them, and he knew the whole area inside out. Nothing further was said.

Night was falling as the aircraft touched down at an airfield in the London area, possibly Northolt. Nothing had been arranged for the two Merchant Navy officers, who made their own way into central London to try to find accommodation for the night. Looking like a couple of tramps with their ill-fitting clothes, and Mason's hands covered in by now blackened bandages, this proved to be no easy task. Hour after hour they spent knocking on doors looking for rooms, and in what must have been an amusing conversation at cross-purposes, it transpired that one house they tried was a brothel! Finally they found a couple of rooms in 'a real dump', but by then they were far too tired to care[8]. As if to add insult to injury, shortly after arriving in the U.K. Captain Mason was diagnosed as suffering from septic periostitis – a complication arising from septic insect bites

112

– and ordered to rest for two weeks. He may not have remained in Malta for long, but evidently long enough to receive the attentions of the sandfly!

For his part in bringing *Ohio* through, Dudley Mason was awarded the George Cross, the highest decoration available to a civilian, and equivalent to the military Victoria Cross. Captain Mason was the first merchant seaman to receive the decoration, and was subsequently also awarded the Lloyd's War Medal for Bravery at Sea.

From July 1945 until May 1946, Eagle Oil loaned Mason to the Ministry of War Transport, who based him in Naples as Superintendent in charge of all fresh water shipments into Italy. On his return to Eagle, he served a further five years as a Master at sea, until, in August 1951, he came ashore to take up the post of Marine Superintendent for the company. Captain Mason retired in 1958, a year before Eagle Oil was absorbed by Shell.

Dudley Mason passed away in April 1987, mourners at his funeral including the High Commissioner for Malta, the Commander in Chief Portsmouth, and representatives from Shell and the HMS *Manchester* Association, of which he had been made an honorary life member a few years previously[9].

James Wyld had the distinction of being the first Merchant Navy officer to be awarded the Distinguished Service Order, usually a military decoration. Wyld came ashore for special duties with Eagle Oil in 1943, was appointed Assistant Engineer Superintendent in 1945, and Engineer Superintendent in 1951, a post held until his retirement in 1958.

★　　★　　★　　★

On 26 September 1942 the crew of *Ohio* suffered their second fatality when Assistant Steward Raymond Banner died in hospital in Malta of peritonitis. One more name to be added to the estimated 350 merchant seamen from *Pedestal* who would never see home again.

## Notes

[1]　*SC88/5*, File 2, Shell Archive, Shell Centre, London.
[2]　*DESTROYER CAPTAIN*, Roger Hill, Wm. Kimber, 1975, p. 86.
[3]　*Ibid.*, p. 90.
[4]　*Ibid.*, p. 91.
[5]　Lieutenant Keith Frost, in correspondence with the author.

6    Eagle Oil memorandum dated 1 September 1942, *SC88/5*, File 1, Shell Archive, Shell Centre, London.

7    www.USMM.org.

8    Mrs Patricia Davis, Captain Mason's stepdaughter, in correspondence with the author.

9    *Ibid.*

# CHAPTER NINE

# EPILOGUE

## I

During his visit to President Roosevelt in June 1942, in addition to the many momentous matters under discussion, Prime Minister Churchill received the unwelcome news that Tobruk, Britain's only remaining bastion in Libya, had surrendered. This did nothing to enhance Malta's already isolated position, and on his return to Britain Churchill received a rough ride from press and parliament over the apparently deteriorating war situation, although his premiership was never seriously in doubt. Churchill determined that the only way to sort out what he perceived to be a lacklustre chain of command in the Middle East was to fly to Egypt. However, with the destruction of Convoy PQ17 in July, the Prime Minister was reminded both by Russian Ambassador Maisky, and an uncompromising telegram from Premier Stalin on the 23rd of that month, of the deepening distrust held by the Soviet authorities over exactly how committed Britain and her allies were to the defeat of Germany. Keeping the Russians onboard was of the utmost importance, therefore Churchill resolved that following his expedition to Cairo, scheduled for early August, he must fly on to Moscow for a face-to-face meeting with Stalin.

On the evening of 2 August, *Pedestal* departed the Clyde; and on 4 August, Churchill arrived in Cairo. Taking some days to decide what form the shake-up of Middle East command would take, on the night of the 10th, the Prime Minister boarded his aircraft and took off for Moscow, via a brief stopover in Persia (Iran).

Having spent a night in Teheran, Churchill arrived in Moscow on 12 August for a stay of several days, and a series of meetings, the success or failure of which seemed to depend as much upon the mood of his mercurial host as the subjects under discussion – which ranged from a likely date for the opening of a second front in Europe, to Operation *Torch,* and inevitably the convoys. At their last meeting, beginning on the evening of the 15th and going on well into the morning of the 16th, Stalin was scathing over the fate of PQ17 and virtually accused the Royal Navy of cowardice in leaving the merchantmen to their fate. Having been kept appraised of the progress of *Pedestal,* Churchill, in a response so animated that interpreters had more trouble than usual keeping up with him (interpretation was apparently not of the highest order for any of the meetings), was able to use the Malta convoy to illustrate how both the Royal and Merchant Navies were prepared to fight their way through against tremendous odds.

With or without the inadequacies of the translation, Stalin is unlikely to have been impressed by Churchill's famous rhetoric, though he does appear to have been taken by the British Prime Minister's unwavering determination to defeat Hitler, and by the time they parted that morning of 16 August there seems to have been a meeting of minds of sorts between the two improbable allies.

# II

With the arrival in Malta of the five merchant ships from *Pedestal* 50,000 tons (50,800 tonnes) of stores, supplies and ammunition were landed, plus the final cargo out-turns from *Ohio*:

| | |
|---|---|
| Kerosene | 1,430 tons (1,453 tonnes) |
| Fuel Oil | 8,695 tons (8,834 tonnes) |
| Bunker fuel | 902 tons (916 tonnes) |
| Lubricating Oil | 2,000 gallons (9,092 litres) |

Despite her travails, the ship landed the great majority of her cargo, losing 1,705.6 tons (1,733 tonnes) of diesel oil and 464 tons (471 tonnes) of kerosene to enemy action.

Malta immediately returned to the offensive, and the effects were dramatic. In the month of August, Axis supplies unloaded in Libya fell to 29,255 tons, (29,723 tonnes), a loss rate of 25 per cent, while supplies of fuel fell to 22,500 tons (22,860 tonnes) at a loss rate of 41 per cent. Not one tanker despatched from Italy to Libya arrived undamaged, and in total some 200,000 tons (203,200 tonnes) of Axis merchant shipping were sunk or put out of action. Stalled by the British defensive positions at El Alamein, Rommel demanded ever more vehicles, supplies and petrol – always more petrol. In an effort to counter the increased activity from Malta, additional Italian warships were assigned to convoy protection, resulting in an improvement in the September figures to 46,465 tons (47,208 tonnes) of supplies and 31,061 tons (31,558 tonnes) of fuel, at an overall loss rate of 20 per cent. This proved to be a false dawn however, as by October supplies landed for the Italian-German Panzer Armee fell back to 33,390 tons (33,924 tonnes) plus a disastrous 12,308 tons (12,505 tonnes) of fuel, at a staggering overall loss rate of 44 per cent[1].

★    ★    ★    ★

In an enormous blow to the British campaign in the Western Desert, Lieutenant General Richard O'Connor, whose destruction of the vastly superior Italian army of Graziani would have thrown the Axis out of Libya in 1940 had his army not been disbanded, was captured on 6 April 1941. Thereafter, despite often being numerically superior to the Panzer Armee and benefiting from the support of the superb Desert Air Force, the Eighth Army suffered a series of reverses, culminating in the capture of Tobruk and Rommel's invasion of Egypt. Nevertheless, Auchinleck brought a measure of stability and is credited with drawing up plans subsequently used in large measure for the defeat of Rommel at El Alamein. It has been suggested that Churchill's reasons for replacing the senior officers of Middle East command were as much political as military, as he believed (with some justification) that setbacks in the desert reflected badly on his ability as a war leader. It seems certain that the Prime Minister reached his decision to replace Auchinleck with General Alexander as C-in-C Middle East before ever arriving in Egypt, and had as his first choice for field command of the Eighth Army Lieutenant General W.H.E. Gott. Gott was something of a legend in the Eighth Army, commanded XIII Corps, and was an experienced desert warrior, although to Auchinleck he seemed tired. This would scarcely be surprising as he arrived in Egypt in 1939 and held combat command from the start of the desert campaign. What manner of army commander Gott would have made will never be known as he was killed on 7 August, en route for Cairo, when the aircraft in which he travelled was shot down. Command of the Eighth Army thereupon fell to Churchill's second choice, Lieutenant General Bernard Law Montgomery.

Montgomery took command on 12 August, by which time Rommel's plans for his next assault, a 'right hook' flank attack in the hope of dislodging the Eighth Army from its positions, were well advanced. Gifted an opportunity to catch the incoming commander flat-footed, Rommel let the days slip by as he waited for resupply until *'By the end of August the urgently needed supplies of ammunition and petrol . . . had still not arrived. The full moon, absolutely vital to our operation, was already on the wane'*[2]. Finally unable to wait any longer, the Desert Fox attacked on 31 August, but by 3 September had been driven back virtually to where he started. The Battle of Alam Halfa proved to be Rommel's desert swansong, and he blamed for the defeat:

1. The strength of the British positions (Note that while the Field Marshal waited for supplies that would never come, Montgomery received Ultra decrypts giving details of his illustrious opponent's plans and had time to prepare).

2. Air superiority of the Desert Air Force.

3. *'The petrol, which was a necessary condition for the implementation of our plans, did not arrive'*[3].

As already noted, Malta's return to the offensive marked a significant decline in the ability of the Italian navy to get supplies across the Mediterranean to the Panzer Armee, and it is estimated that between the arrival of *Pedestal* and the opening of the Battle of El Alamein on 23 October 1942, some 300,000 tons (304,800 tonnes)[4] of Axis shipping were sunk by aircraft, submarines and surface ships based at Malta.

With Malta held and Rommel driven back in defeat at El Alamein, the *Torch* landings in French Morocco and Algeria took place on 8 November 1942. There was still plenty of fight left in the Panzer Armee (as U.S. troops in the Kasserine Pass discovered in February 1943), but attacked in overwhelming force from both east and west their days were numbered, and on 9 March 1943 Field Marshal Rommel left North Africa for good. By mid-May, Axis resistance in the desert had crumbled, Allied armies taking over a quarter of a million prisoners of war. The end of the campaign opened the way for an Allied assault on what Winston Churchill termed the 'soft underbelly' of Nazi-occupied Europe, through Sicily and into Italy, which surrendered in September 1943. Nevertheless, German armies in Italy fought on and the fierce battles around Monte Cassino, Anzio and Salerno still lay ahead.

# III

Some time after *Pedestal*, Ray Morton signed T124X articles, enabling merchant navy crewmen to serve aboard Royal Navy ships under RN command. Ray served aboard the escort/assault carrier HMS *Ameer*, part of South-East Asia Command, and saw action against the Japanese off Burma, Malaya and Sumatra.

Despite the privations suffered by the British merchant marine during the Second World War, governments of both political hues since the war have seen fit to deny 'veteran' status to the officers and men of the merchant navy, including those who signed T124 and T124X Articles and served aboard Royal Navy ships. Incredibly, it is only since 1999 that representatives of the merchant navy have been allowed to take part in the annual Remembrance Day march past at the Cenotaph in London.

In recognition of the vital part played by the Arctic supply convoys, the Russian administration minted a commemorative medal for the Allied seamen who fought them through, but the Ministry of Defence steadfastly refuses to allow British merchant seamen to accept it. Unlike their colleagues in the U.S., Canadian, Australian, and New Zealand merchant service, who have been accorded 'veteran' status, British merchant seamen are regarded by their political 'masters' as civilians in reserved occupations doing their peacetime jobs. It is long past time that small-minded, mean-spirited political and bureaucratic denial of the vital part played by the merchant navy – <u>without whom the war could not have been won</u> – was rectified.

★　　★　　★　　★

It was 19 September 1946, and a sleek grey Royal Navy destroyer waited on station ten miles from Malta. In Grand Harbour, tugs fussed around two rusted hulks, the remains of what had once been a tanker. This was *Ohio*, and as she came one last time to the open sea no bands or cheering crowds marked her passing, for momentous events had overtaken her epic voyage – the fall of Hitler, the defeat of Japan, the Atom Bomb . . . But for a moment in that great conflict, the fate of a small island, the lynchpin of the campaign in the Mediterranean and possibly much more, depended upon this fine ship and her truly exceptional crew.

Having successfully discharged her cargo, *Ohio* finally broke her back completely. The two halves were drydocked, bulkheads made watertight and attempts made to effect repair, but facilities and technical expertise for joining the ship together simply did not exist in Malta, and the cost of towage to Gibraltar or Alexandria was prohibitive. Subsequently, *Ohio* found employment as a store ship and as a billet for Yugoslav troops – leading to erroneous newspaper reports in Europe and the United States that 'the ship which saved Malta' had been rebuilt and sold to the Yugoslavs.

With the war's end she was of no further use, and now the tugs brought her at last to the end of her voyage, cast off from her shattered hull and returned to Malta. Standing off from the wreck the destroyer loaded armour-piercing shell and opened fire. The after part of the tanker, so ravaged by air attack, soon succumbed to this new onslaught and sank, but the less damaged forepart proved stubborn to the end, resisting salvo after salvo. Inevitably the pounding told at last, and with her bridge superstructure destroyed and temporary repairs to the old torpedo damage giving way, the graceful schooner bow finally pointed reluctantly to the sky and *Ohio* slipped silently beneath the warm waters of the Mediterranean.

## Notes

[1]    *THE ITALIAN NAVY IN WORLD WAR II*, Commander (R) Marc' Antonio Bragadin, United States Naval Institute, 1957, p. 216.
[2]    *ROMMEL, In His Own Words*, ed. Dr. John Pimlott, Greenhill Books, Lionel Leventhal Ltd., 1994, p. 132.
[3]    *Ibid.*, p. 134.
[4]    *CONVOY*, documentary, Channel 4 Television.

# APPENDIX 1

# T.T. *OHIO*

## OUTLINE DETAILS AND TRIALS INFORMATION*

*BUILDERS*:                          Sun Shipbuilding & Drydock Co.,
                                     Chester, Pa.

*BUILT*:
Keel laid:                           7 September 1939.
Launched:                            20 April 1940.
Delivered to Texaco:                 22 June 1940.

*TONNAGES*:
Loaded displacement:                 19,320 tons (19,629 tonnes).
Light displacement:                  5,170 tons (5,253 tonnes).
Deadweight:                          14,130 tons (14,356 tonnes).
Gross:                               9,264 tons (9,412 tonnes)
Net:                                 5,438 tons (5,525 tonnes).

*DIMENSIONS*:
Length overall:                      513'10" (156.6m).
Moulded beam:                        68'0" (20.7m).
Depth:                               36'0" (11m).
Summer freeboard:                    7'8" (2.3m).
Summer loaded draft:                 28'5 7/8" (8.68m).

*CLASSIFICATION:*                    Highest Lloyds & American Bureau
                                     of Shipping.

* Chevron Texaco archive, U.S.A.

| | |
|---|---|
| *CARGO TANKS:* | 9 centre, 8 large and 16 small wing tanks. |
| *PUMPS:* | Four Kinney Heliquad capable of 2,000 barrels per hour, plus four Kinney Heliquad luboil cargo pumps capable of 1,000 barrels per hour. Single pump-room abaft the bridge. |
| *MAIN ENGINE:* | Double-reduction geared steam turbines, built by Westinghouse Elec. Mfg. Co. |
| Turbines r.p.m: | High-pressure turbine, 5,978. Low-pressure turbine, 4,484. |
| Shaft Horse Power: | 9,000 @ 90 shaft rpm. |
| *BOILERS:* | Two Babcock & Wilcox with economisers & superheaters. |
| Type: | Two drum marine. |
| Working Pressure: | 450 lbs. psi (450 lb/6.45 sq.cm.) |
| *PROPELLER:* | Single four-blade solid manganese bronze. |
| Diameter: | 20'6" (6.2m). |
| Pitch: | 19.67' (5.99m). |
| *COMPLEMENT:* | Forty-one (standard peacetime). |

# SPEED DATA ~ STANDARDISATION TRIALS

18 June 1940 – water temperature 220°F oxygen zero.

| Run no. | Time | r.p.m. | Average r.p.m. | Rated s.h.p. | Developed s.h.p. | Speed in knots | Average Speed in knots |
|---------|------|--------|----------------|--------------|------------------|----------------|------------------------|
| 1. | 7.15am | 63 | | | | 13.850 | |
| | | | 63.5 | 3,000 | 3,200 | | 12.45 |
| 2. | 7.30am | 64 | | | | 11.053 | |
| 3. | 7.50am | 76 | | | | 15.96 | |
| | | | 76.15 | 5,200 | 5,450 | | 15.01 |
| 4. | 8.15am | 76.3 | | | | 14.06 | |
| 5. | 10.15am | 91 | | | | 16.21 | |
| | | | 90.65 | 9,000 | 9,220 | | 17.2 |
| 6. | 10.30am | 90.3 | | | | 18.20 | |
| 7. | 11.05am | 93.7 | | | | 15.48 | |
| | | | 93.5 | 10,000 | 10,200 | | 17.355 |
| 8. | 11.20am | 93.4 | | | | 19.23 | |

*Details runs no. 7 & 8 / 93 rpm.*

| | |
|---|---|
| Boiler steam recapitulation: | 93 rpm trial (about 10,000 s.h.p.) |
| Total steam 104,100 lb/hr | |
| Main Turbines | 73,030 lb/hr |
| Generators | 3,010 lb/hr |
| Air Ejector/Gland Steam | 415 lb/hr |
| Main B.F. pump | 4,575 lb/hr |
| General service & ballast pump | 1,720 lb/hr |
| Steering engine & deck machinery | 13,900 lb/hr |
| Losses | 1,725 lb/hr |

| | |
|---|---|
| Make-up feedwater | 5,725 lb/hr |
| Totals: | |
| | |
| 104,100 lb/hr | 104,100 lb/hr |
| Actual propeller speed | 93.6 rpm. |
| Average ship speed (two runs) | 17.35 knots/hr. |
| Developed s.h.p. based on h.p. curve | 10,200 s.h.p/hr. |
| Lbs/kilos of oil used | 7,425 lb/hr (3,368 kg/hr). |
| All-purpose fuel rate | 0.728 lb/s.h.p./hr. (0.330 kg). |
| Assumed boiler efficiency | 85.35%. |
| Draft forward | 28'0" (8.5m). |
| Draft aft | 28'0" (8.5m). |
| Oil used per 1,000 lb of steam | 71.25 lb per hour (32.32 kg). |

# AUXILIARY STEERING GEAR TEST.

VESSEL S.S. "OHIO" — OFF OVERFALLS LIGHT SHIP. DATE JUNE-18-1940

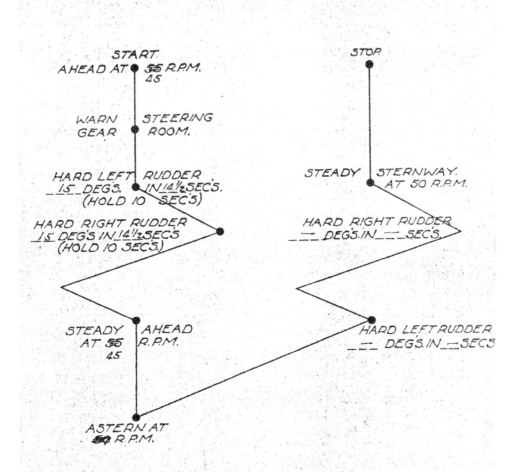

START.
AHEAD AT 55 R.P.M.
        45

STOP.

WARN   STEERING
GEAR   ROOM.

STEADY   STERNWAY.
         AT 50 R.P.M.

HARD LEFT RUDDER
15 DEGS. IN 14½ SECS.
(HOLD 10 SECS)

HARD RIGHT RUDDER
15 DEGS IN 14½ SECS
(HOLD 10 SECS.)

HARD RIGHT RUDDER
— DEGS. IN — SECS.

STEADY   AHEAD
AT 55    R.P.M.
   45

HARD LEFT RUDDER
— DEGS. IN — SECS

ASTERN AT
50 R.P.M.

SUN SHIPBUILDING & DRYDOCK CO.
AUXILIARY   STEERING
        GEAR  TEST.
APPROVED. _____ CHIEF ENGR.

SK. No.

125

# TRIALS MANOEUVRING DIAGRAM.

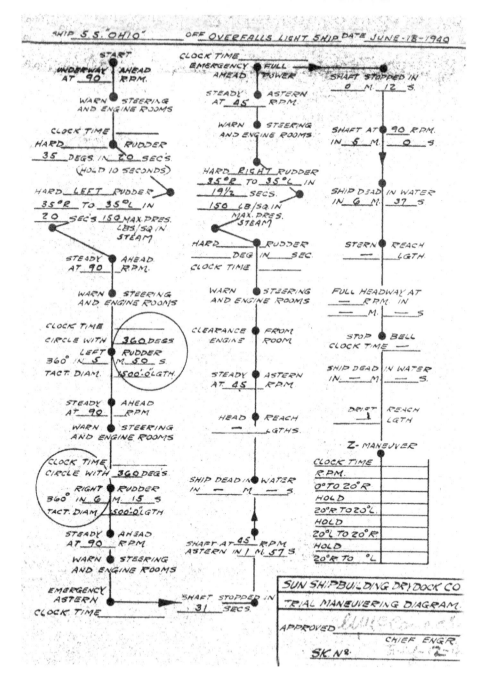

# CREW LISTS

## U.S. CREW FROM HOUSTON, TEXAS, TO BOWLING ON THE CLYDE, MAY/JUNE 1942.

Captain Sverre Petersen, Master.

Ralph L. Kuhn, Chief Mate.

Ole Halvorsen, Second Mate.

Charles G. Andersen, Third Mate.

Keith G. Martin, Radio Operator.

Earl W. Arnold, Maintenance Foreman.

Paul M. Shields, A.B.

William P. Wells, A.B.

Tilden T. Anderson, A.B.

Robert E. Morris, A.B.

Frank E. McCoy, A.B.

James E. Callum, A.B.

Alfred E. Jameson, Deck Maintenance.

John C. Tuckendorf, O.S.

Oscar T. Palman, O.S.

Hillery J. Ardoin, O.S.

Virgil J. Bush, Chief Engineer.

Carl Barth, First Assistant Engineer.

James Murphy, Second Assistant Engineer.

Edward J. Doherty, Third Assistant Engineer.

John B. Hamilton, Oiler/Machinist.

Milton H. King, First Pumps.

George W. Ash, Second Pumps.

Jack Bradley, Oiler.

Edward Hamme, Oiler.

John F. Dixon, Oiler.

Ray J. Daigle, Fireman.

Harold J. Train, Fireman.

Dennis P. Dantz, Fireman.

Luther L. Easby, Jr.

Albert W. Ainsley.

Edwin F. Nixon.

George Nicholas, Steward.

Francis Crowe, First Cook.

Albert T. Reviere, Second Cook.

Clement Fantenot, Galleyman.

Harold O'Rourke, Messman.

Leslie L. Traylen, Officers' Mess.

Jefferson Guillery, Petty Officers' Mess.

Clive Stafford, Messman.

Russel L. Fantment, Messman.

John Fay, Deck Maintenance.

Silvio Rama, Deck Boy.

# U.K. CREW AS EMBARKED ON THE CLYDE FOR THE VOYAGE TO MALTA, AUGUST 1942.

*(Decorations awarded for* Pedestal *in italics).*

Captain Dudley William Mason, Master, Westward Ho!, Devon. *George Cross. Lloyds War Medal.*

Douglas Hunter Gray, Chief Officer, Edinburgh. *DSC.*

Hector James McGilligan, Second Officer, Kirriemuir. *DSC.*

Joseph Ross Stephen, Third Officer, Backmuir, nr. Dundee. *DSC.* MBE. Lloyds War Medal.

Robert William Wilkinson, Apprentice, London.

Henry Howard Bulmer, Apprentice, Yorkshire.

James Wyld, Chief Engineer, Glasgow. *DSO.*

Henry Noël Buddle, Second Engineer, Falmouth.

Leonard Victor Grinstead, Third Engineer, Birkenhead. MBE.

Thomas Purvis Murray, Fourth Engineer, Newcastle upon Tyne. *DSC.*

William Stevly Crow, Junior Engineer, Glasgow.

William Shaw Smith, Junior Engineer, Clydebank.

Henry Sless, Junior Engineer, Glasgow. *DSC.*

John B. Higgins, Electrician, Paisley.

Allan Collins, Chief Radio Officer, Cardiff.

Dennis Smith, Second Radio Officer, Kent.

J.C. McLaren, Third Radio Officer, Aberdeen.

Robert Charles Horton, Carpenter, London.

Horace A. Thacker, Boatswain, Port Talbot.

Thomas Leech, Storekeeper, London.

Alexander Collins, Pumpman, Surrey.

Robert Henry Watson, Pumpman, South Shields.

Francis Watson Meeks, Chief Steward, South Shields. *DSM.*

John D. Stephens, Second Steward, Liverpool.

John Church, Assistant Steward, Glasgow.

Raymond V. Morton, Assistant Steward, County Durham.

Raymond Banner, Assistant Steward, Methil. Died in hospital in Malta.

James Henry Potts, Chief Cook, Dumfriesshire.

Leslie Woolley, Second Cook, Liverpool.

Alfred J. Byrne, Crew Pantryman, Elgin.

Thomas Mulholland, Crew Pantryman, Dumbartonshire.

Mario Guidotti, Galley Boy, Glasgow.

Hugh Blane, Able Seaman, Paisley.

Hector McNeil, Able Seaman, Isle of Barra.

George McCole, Able Seaman, Glasgow.

R. Francey, Able Seaman, Glasgow.

A.J. Allen, Able Seaman, Chalfont St. Giles.

D.W. Donald, Able Seaman, c/o P.W.D. Port Elizabeth.

Allan Shaw, Ordinary Seaman, Wetherby, Yorkshire.

Kenneth Arundel, Ordinary Seaman, Castleford.

H. Cooper, Ordinary Seaman, Rainham, Essex.

K. Paterson, Ordinary Seaman, N. Boisdale, S. Uist.

A. MacDonald, Ordinary Seaman, Ardnastruban, N. Uist.

W. McLaughlin, Greaser, Glasgow. *DSM.*

W.J. McConalogue, Greaser, Glasgow. *DSM.*

J. McConalogue, Greaser, Glasgow. *DSM.*

T. Cameron, Greaser, Blantyre.

J. Gubbins, Greaser, Falkirk.

A. Woods, Greaser, Glasgow. *DSM.*

J. Marmion, Fireman, Glasgow.

P. Dolan, Fireman, Glasgow. *DSM.*

A. Hodgson, Fireman, Glasgow.

R. Lennon, Fireman, Ardrossan.

Alexander Pilling, Gunlayer Royal Navy, in command of RN Gunners (signed on as a Deckhand to comply with Board of Trade regulations), Blackpool. *DSM.*

David Pickwell, RN Gunner/Deckhand, Stamford.

Arthur C. Swell, RN Gunner/Deckhand, Seven Kings, Ilford, Essex.

James Ross, RN Gunner/Deckhand, Bo'ness.

Christopher Dunne, RN Gunner/Deckhand, County Meath.

Edward W. Rimmer, RN Gunner/Deckhand, Preston, Lancashire.

Reginald La Bern, Bombardier in command of the contingent of army gunners (signed on as a Deckhand), London.

Alexander Marno, Army Gunner/Deckhand, Belfast.

Gregory Haggerty, Army Gunner/Deckhand, Burnbrae, Alexandria.

Thomas Pedley, Army Gunner/Deckhand, Wakefield.

Peter Brown, Army Gunner/Deckhand, St. Helens. Died of wounds, buried at sea.

Stanley Hawkins, Army Gunner/Deckhand, Leigh, Lancashire.

Bernard J. O'Hagan, Army Gunner/Deckhand, Glasgow.

Albert Lamb, Army Gunner/Deckhand, Loch Maben, Dumfries.

H. Bates, Army Gunner/Deckhand, Liverpool.

Edward Smith, Army Gunner/Deckhand, Lancashire.

R. Welsh, Army Gunner/Deckhand, Ayr.

W.H. Hands, Army Gunner/Deckhand, Manchester.

G. Hitton, Army Gunner/Deckhand, Manchester.

D.E. Barton, Army Gunner/Deckhand, Norfolk.

A. Bechelli, Army Gunner/Deckhand, Ilford, Essex.

A.J. Butcher, Army Gunner/Deckhand, London.

L.N. Clarke, Army Gunner/Deckhand, Thames Ditton.

J.R. Lemin, Army Gunner/Deckhand, N. Lancashire.

# APPENDIX 3

# OUTLINE SPECIFICATIONS[1] OF MERCHANT SHIPS ENGAGED IN *PEDESTAL*

(details are approximate)

**Almeria Lykes**

U.S. Flag.

Built Federal Shipbuilding & Drydock Co., Kearney, New Jersey, 1942.

12,830 tons deadweight (13,035 tonnes) on 29'2" (8.85m) loaded draft.

7,821 tons gross (7,946 tonnes).

Length 492'0" overall (150m) x 69'7" breadth (21.19m).

Main engines steam turbines designed to achieve a maximum loaded speed of 16 knots.

Owners Lykes Bros. Steamship Co. Inc., New Orleans.

**Brisbane Star**

British flag.

Built Cammel Laird & Co., Birkenhead, 1936.

11,519 tons deadweight (11,703 tonnes) on 30'11" (9.4m) loaded draft.

11,076 tons gross (11,253 tonnes).

Length 548'11" overall (167.3m) x 70'3" breadth (21.4m)

Diesel main engines geared to twin propeller shafts.

Maximum loaded speed 16 knots.

Owners Union Cold Storage Co. Ltd., part of the Blue Star Line Group, London.

### Clan Ferguson

British Flag.

Built Greenock Dockyard Co. Ltd., Greenock, 1938.

10,160 tons deadweight (10,322 tonnes) on 28'4" (8.63m) loaded draft.

7,347 tons gross (7,464 tonnes).

484'6" length overall (147.7m) x 63'0" breadth (19.2m).

Steam reciprocating main engines with exhaust turbines, geared to twin propeller shafts.

Maximum loaded speed 16 knots.

Owners The Clan Line Steamers Ltd., London.

### Deucalion

British flag.

Built R. & W. Hawthorn, Leslie & Co., Hebburn, 1930.

8,930 tons deadweight (9,073 tonnes) on 28'6" (8.7m) loaded draft.

7,740 tons gross (7,864 tonnes).

478'0" length overall (145.7m) x 59'5" breadth (18.2m).

Diesel engines geared to twin propeller shafts.

Maximum loaded speed 16 knots.

Owners Ocean Steamship Co. Ltd., part of the Alfred Holt (Blue Funnel) Group, Liverpool.

### Dorset

British flag.

Built Workman Clarke (1928) Ltd., Belfast, 1934.

13,650 tons deadweight (13,864 tonnes) on 32'6" (9.9m) loaded draft.

10,624 tons gross (10,794 tonnes).

513'0" length overall (156.4m) x 68.8' (20.9m) breadth.

Diesel engines geared to twin propeller shafts.

Maximum loaded speed 16 knots.

Owners Federal Steam Navigation Co., London.

### *Empire Hope*[2]

British flag.

Built Harland & Wolff Ltd., Belfast, 1941.

Cargo capacity made up almost entirely of refrigerated space, for the transportation of meat and other perishable goods.

12,688 tons gross (12,891 tonnes).

521.4' length overall (158.9m) x 70.4' breadth (21.4m).

Diesel engines geared to twin propeller shafts.

Maximum loaded speed 16 knots.

Built to a design by the Shaw, Savill & Albion Company, London, for the Ministry of War Transport and placed under Shaw Savill management.

### *Glenorchy*

British flag.

Built Taikoo Dockyard & Engineering Co., Hong Kong, 1939.

9,500 tons deadweight (9,652 tonnes) on 30'7" (9.3m) loaded draft.

8,982 tons gross (9,125 tonnes).

507'0" length overall (154.5m) x 66'5" breadth (20.3m).

Diesel engines geared to twin propeller shafts.

Maximum loaded speed 18 knots.

Owners Glen Line Ltd., London.

### Melbourne Star

British flag.

Built Cammel Laird & Co. Ltd., Birkenhead, 1936.

11,800 tons deadweight (11,989 tonnes) on 29'8" (9.04m) loaded draft.

12,891 tons gross (13,097 tonnes).

542'10" length overall (165.4m) x 70'5" breadth (21.5m).

Diesel engines geared to twin propeller shafts.

Maximum loaded speed 16 knots.

Owners Union Cold Storage Co. Ltd., part of the Blue Star Line Group, London.


### Port Chalmers (Commodore's ship).

British flag.

Built Swan, Hunter, & Wigham Richardson Ltd., Wallsend, Sunderland, 1933.

11,610 tons deadweight (11,786 tonnes) on 29'10" (9.08m) loaded draft.

8,535 tons gross (8,672 tonnes).

506'10" length overall (154.51m) x 65'4" breadth (19.9m).

Diesel engines geared to twin propeller shafts.

Maximum loaded speed 15 knots.

Owners Port Line Ltd., London, part of the Cunard Group.


### Rochester Castle

British flag.

Built Harland & Wolff Ltd., Belfast, 1937.

9,258 tons deadweight on 29'2" (8.9m) loaded draft.

7,795 tons gross (7,920 tonnes).

474'2" length overall (144.5m) x 63'4" breadth (19.3m).

Diesel engine, single screw.

Maximum loaded speed 16.5 knots.

Owners The Union-Castle Mail Steamship Co. Ltd., London.

### Santa Elisa

U.S. flag.

Built Federal Shipbuilding & Drydock Co., Kearney, New Jersey, 1940.

9,020 tons deadweight (9,164 tonnes) on 25'9" loaded draft (7.8m).

8,380 tons gross (8,514 tonnes).

459'3" length overall (140m) x 63'2" breadth (19.2m).

Steam turbines geared to single propeller shaft.

Maximum loaded speed 16 knots.

Owners Grace Line Inc., New York.


### Waimarama

British flag.

Built Harland & Wolff Ltd., Belfast, 1938.

13,000 tons deadweight (13,208 tonnes) on 29'7" (9m) loaded draft.

12,843 tons gross (13,048 tonnes).

535'6" length overall (163.2m) x 70'5" breadth (21.4m).

Diesel engines geared to twin propeller shafts.

Maximum loaded speed 16.5 knots.

Owners Shaw, Savill & Albion Co. Ltd., London.


### Wairangi

British flag.

Built Harland & Wolff Ltd., Govan, Glasgow, 1935.

12,313 tons deadweight (12,510 tonnes) on 29'8" (9m) loaded draft.

10,796 tons gross (10,969 tonnes).

535'6" length overall (163.2m) x 70'5" breadth (21.4m).

Diesel engines geared to twin propeller shafts.

Maximum loaded speed 17 knots.

Owners Shaw, Savill & Albion Co. Ltd., London.

## Notes

1    *THE WORLD'S MERCHANT FLEETS 1939*, Roger Jordan, Chatham Publishing, 1999.
2    *THE EMPIRE SHIPS*, W.H. Mitchell & L.A. Sawyer, Lloyds of London Press Ltd., 1990, p. 183.

# APPENDIX 4

## (A) COMPOSITION OF NAVAL FORCES ENGAGED IN THE ESCORT OF *PEDESTAL*

### FORCE Z (escort from the U.K. as far as Cape Bon)

**Battleships:**

| | |
|---|---|
| Nelson | (Flagship) Senior Officer Vice Admiral Sir E.N. Syfret, CB. |
| | Captain H.B. Jacomb. |
| Rodney | Captain J.W. Rivett-Carnac, DSC. |

**Aircraft Carriers:**

| | |
|---|---|
| Victorious | Flag Officer, Aircraft Carriers, Rear Admiral Sir A. Lyster, CB. |
| | Captain H.C. Bovell. |
| Indomitable | Captain T.H. Troubridge. |
| Eagle | Captain L.D. Mackintosh, DSC. |
| Furious | Captain T.O. Bulteel. |

(plus on attachment for Operation *Berserk* Aircraft carrier *Argus*, Captain G.T. Philip, DSC.)

**Light Cruisers:**

| | |
|---|---|
| Phoebe | Captain C.P. Frend. |
| Sirius | Captain P.W. Brooking. |
| Charybdis | Captain G.A. Voelcker. |

**Destroyers:**

| | |
|---|---|
| Laforey | Captain (D) Nineteenth Destroyer Flotilla, Captain R. Hutton. |
| Antelope | Lieutenant Commander E.N. Sinclair. |
| Eskimo | Commander E.G. Le Geyt, DSC. |
| Ithuriel | Lieutenant Commander D.H. Maitland-Makgill-Crichton, DSC. |

| | |
|---|---|
| *Lightning* | Commander H.G. Walters. |
| *Lookout* | Lieutenant Commander C.P. Brown. |
| *Quentin* | Lieutenant Commander A.H. Noble, DSC. |
| *Somali* | Commander E.N. Currey, DSC. |
| *Tartar* | Commander St. J. R. Tyrwhitt, DSC. |
| *Vansittart* | Lieutenant Commander T. Johnston, DSC. |
| *Wishart* | Commander H.G. Scott. |
| *Westcott* | Commander I.H. Bockett-Pugh, DSO. |
| *Wrester* | Lieutenant R.W. Lacon, DSC. |
| *Wilton* | Lieutenant A.P. Northey, DSC. |
| *Zetland* | Lieutenant J.V. Wilkenson. |

## Additional destroyers on attachment from Western Approaches Command

| | |
|---|---|
| *Amazon* | Lieutenant Commander Lord Teynham. |
| *Keppel* | Commander J.H. Broome. |
| *Malcolm* | Commander A.B. Russell. |
| *Venomous* | Commander H.W. Falcon-Steward. |
| *Vidette* | Lieutenant Commander E.N. Walmsley, DSC. |
| *Wolverine* | Lieutenant Commander P.W. Gretton, OBE, DSC. |

## FORCE X –under the command of Vice Admiral Syfret until Cape Bon, thereafter designated escort to take the convoy on to Malta.

### *Light Cruisers:*

| | |
|---|---|
| *Nigeria* | Flagship Tenth Cruiser Squadron, Rear Admiral H.M. Burrough, CB, DSO. Captain S.H. Paton. |
| *Cairo* | Captain (Acting) C.C. Hardy, DSO. |
| *Kenya* | Captain A.S. Russell. |
| *Manchester* | Captain H. Drew, DSC. |

### *Destroyers:*

| | |
|---|---|
| *Ashanti* | Captain (D) Sixth Destroyer Flotilla, Commander R.G. Onslow, DSO. |
| *Bicester* | Lieutenant Commander S.W. Bennets. |
| *Bramham* | Lieutenant E.F. Baines (see page 142) |

| | |
|---|---|
| *Derwent* | Commander R.H. Wright, DSC. |
| *Foresight* | Lieutenant Commander R.A. Fell. |
| *Fury* | Lieutenant Commander C.H. Campbell, DSC. |
| *Icarus* | Lieutenant Commander C.D. Maud, DSC. |
| *Intrepid* | Commander E.A. de W. Kitkat. |
| *Ledbury* | Lieutenant Commander R.P. Hill (see page 143). |
| *Pathfinder* | Commander E.A. Gibbs, DSO. |
| *Penn* | Lieutenant Commander J.H. Swain (see page 144). |

## Force R −fleet tankers for refuelling at sea

| | |
|---|---|
| *Brown Ranger* | Captain D.B. Ralph. |
| *Dingledale* | Captain R.T. Duthie. |

### *Corvettes:*

| | |
|---|---|
| *Coltsfoot* | Temporary Lieutenant The Hon. W.K. Rous, RNVR. |
| *Geranium* | Temporary Lieutenant Commander A. Foxall, RNR. |
| *Jonquil* | Lieutenant Commander R.E. Partington, RD, RNR. |
| *Salvonia* | Temporary Lieutenant G.M. Robinson. |
| *Spirea* | Lieutenant Commander R.S. Miller, DSC, RD, RNR. |

## Force W −fleet tanker on attachment for Operation *Berserk*

| | |
|---|---|
| *Abbeydale* | Captain A. Edwards. |

### *Corvettes:*

| | |
|---|---|
| *Armieira* | Lieutenant M. Todd, RNR. |
| *Burdock* | Lieutenant Commander. E.H. Lynes, RNR. |

**Also on attachment:**

*Destroyers:*

| | |
|---|---|
| Badsworth | Lieutenant G.T. Gray, DSC. |
| Matchless | Lieutenant Commander J. Mowlam. |

*Tug:*

| | |
|---|---|
| Jaunty | Lieutenant Commander H. Osburn, OBE RNR. |

### Seventeenth Minesweeping Flotilla, Malta
### Flotilla Commander H.J. Jerome, RN.

| | |
|---|---|
| Speedy | Commander A.E. Doran. |
| Rye | Lieutenant J.A. Pearson, DSC, RNR (see p. 44). |
| Hebe | Lieutenant Commander G. Mowatt, RD, RNVR. |
| Hythe | Lieutenant Commander L.B. Miller. |

### Third Motor Launch Flotilla, Malta

ML 121   Lieutenant Commander E.J. Strowgler, RNVR, Senior Officer
MLs 126/ 134/135/ 168/459/462.

# (B) OUTLINE DETAILS[1] OF WARSHIPS CLOSELY INVOLVED WITH *OHIO*.

### Type II 'Hunt' class escort destroyers
### Ledbury & Bramham

| | |
|---|---|
| Displacement: | 1,430 tons full load on 10' draft. (1,452 tonnes on 3.05m). |
| Built: | *Ledbury:* Thorneycroft, completed February 1942. *Bramham:* A. Stephen, completed June 1942. |
| Dimensions: | 280' length overall x 31'6" x 17'3". (85.3m x 9.6m x 5.26m). |
| Machinery: | Parsons geared turbines, 19,000 SHP, to twin screw shafts. |
| Speed: | About 25½ knots at full load (27 knots max.) |
| Armament: | Six 4" (101.6mm) HA/LA guns. Four 2pdr (0.91kg) anti-aircraft, single mounting. Two 20mm anti-aircraft, single mounting. Two anti-submarine mortars. 110 depth charges in three racks. |

### 'P' class destroyer
### Penn

| | |
|---|---|
| Displacement: | 2,250 tons full load on 12'3" draft. 2,286 tonnes on 3.73m. |

| Built: | Vickers Armstrong, completed February 1942. |
| --- | --- |
| Dimensions: | 345' length overall x 35' x 20'3". (105m x 10.7m x 6.2m). |
| Machinery: | Parsons geared turbines, 40,000 SHP, to twin screw shafts. |
| Speed: | About 33 knots full load (36.25 knots max.). |
| Armament: | Five 4" (101.6mm) HA/LA guns. Four 2pdr (0.91kg) anti-aircraft, single mounting. Four 20mm anti-aircraft, single mounting. Two 0.303" machine guns, single mounting. Four 21" (533mm) torpedo tubes, single mounting. Four anti-submarine mortars. Seventy depth charges on two racks. |

## 'Bangor' class minesweeper Rye

| Displacement: | 820 tons full load on 10'3" draft. (833 tonnes on 3.12m). |
| --- | --- |
| Built: | Ailsa Shipbuilding, completed November 1941. |
| Dimensions: | 174' length overall x 28'6". (53m x 8.7m). |
| Machinery: | Parsons geared turbines, 2,000 SHP, to twin screw shafts. |

Speed:                          16 knots.

Armament:                       One 12pdr (5.4kg) anti-aircraft.
                                One 2pdr (0.91kg) anti-aircraft.
                                One 20mm anti-aircraft per
                                bridge wing.

## 'Halcyon' class minesweeper/escort sloop
## Speedy

Displacement:                   1,330 tons full load on 9' draft.
                                (1,351 tonnes on 2.74m).

Built:                          Hamilton Shipyard, completed
                                April 1939.

Dimensions:                     245'3" length overall x 33'6"
                                (74.7m x 10.2m).

Machinery:                      Parsons geared turbines, 1,750
                                SHP, geared to twin screw
                                shafts.

Speed:                          16½ knots.

Armament:                       Two 4" (101.6mm) HA/LA
                                guns.
                                Four 0.5" anti-aircraft, single
                                mounting.
                                Four 0.303" machine guns,
                                single mounting.
                                Provision for removal of
                                minesweeping gear and
                                replacement with depth charges.

## Notes

[1]   *BRITISH AND EMPIRE WARSHIPS* of the Second World War, H.T.
      Lenton, Greenhill Books, Lionel Leventhal Ltd., 1998.

# APPENDIX 5

# OUTLINE SPECIFICATIONS OF PRINCIPAL AIRCRAFT TYPES DEPLOYED DURING *PEDESTAL*[1]

## Carrier-based convoy protection fighters

### *Fairey Fulmar Mk. 1*

| | |
|---|---|
| Type: | British-built two-seat navy fighter/bomber. |
| Powerplant: | One 1,080bhp (805kw) Rolls Royce Merlin VIII V12. |
| Performance: | Maximum speed 256mph (412km/h) at 2,500ft (730m), 246mph (396km/h) at sea level. Initial climb rate 1,200ft (366m) per min. Service ceiling 26,000ft (7,925m). Maximum range 830 miles (1,335km). |
| Armament: | Eight 0.303" machine guns in wings. Optional single 0.303" machine gun in rear cockpit. Two 250lb (113kg) bombs under wings. |

### *Grumman Martlet F4F-4*

| | |
|---|---|
| Type: | U.S.-built single-seat navy fighter ('Martlet' was Royal Navy nomenclature for the U.S. Navy's Grumman Wildcat). |
| Powerplant: | One 1,200bhp (895kw) Pratt & |

146

|                | Whitney R-1839-76/86 Twin Wasp fourteen cylinder radial. |
|----------------|---------------------------------|
| Performance:   | Maximum speed 320mph (515km/h) at 18,800ft. 274mph (441km/h) at sea level. Initial climb rate 1,950ft (594m) per min. Service ceiling 34,900ft (10,637m). Normal range 770 miles (1,239km). |
| Armament:      | Four 0.50" machine guns in wings. Provision for two 259lb (113kg) bombs under wings. |

### *Sea Hurricane Mk IIC[2]*

| Type:          | British-built single-seat navy fighter. |
|----------------|---------------------------------|
| Powerplant:    | One 1280bhp (954kw) Rolls Royce Merlin XX. |
| Performance:   | Maximum speed 342mph (550km/h) at 22,000ft (6,706m). Service ceiling 35,600ft (10,851m). Range with internal fuel 460 miles (740km). Range with internal fuel & long-range external tanks 970 miles (1,561km). |
| Armament:      | Four 20mm cannon in wings. |

## Axis aircraft

### *Junkers Ju88A-4*

| Type:          | German-built twin-engined medium bomber/torpedo bomber/fighter. |
|----------------|---------------------------------|
| Powerplant:    | Two 1,340bhp (1,000kw) Junkers Jumo 211F engines. |
| Performance:   | Maximum speed 292mph (470km/h) at 17,390ft. (5,300m). |

147

|                | Initial climb rate 1,312ft (400m) per min. |
|----------------|---|

Initial climb rate 1,312ft (400m) per min.
Service ceiling 26,900ft (8,200m).
Maximum range 1,696 miles (2,730km).

Armament: Maximum bomb load 4,409lb (2,000kg) internally and on under-wing racks.
One 7.92mm machine gun in front cockpit.
One 13mm or two 7.92mm machine guns in nose.
Two 7.92mm machine guns in rear cockpit.
One 13mm or two 7.92mm machine guns in ventral gondola.

### Junkers Ju87D 'Stuka'

Type: Two-seat German-built dive bomber/ground attack aircraft. Operated by both the Luftwaffe and *Regia Aeronautica* in the Mediterranean/North African campaigns.

Powerplant: One 1,400bhp (1,044kw) Junkers Jumo 211J-1 inverted V12.

Performance: Maximum speed 255mph (410km/h) at 12,600ft (3,840m).
Service ceiling 23,915ft (7,290m).
Range with maximum bomb load 620 miles (998km).
Maximum range 954 miles (1,535km).

Armament: Maximum bomb load 3,968lb (1,800kg) under fuselage.
Two 7.9mm machine guns in wings plus two in rear cockpit.
Various gun/bomb options available under wings, up to 1,102lb (500kg).

148

## Savoia-Marchetti SM79/SM84

| | |
|---|---|
| Type: | Italian-built triple-engined four/five seat medium bomber & reconnaissance aircraft. |
| Powerplant: | SM79 Type II/III: three 1,000bhp (746kw) Piaggio P.XI RC 40 fourteen cylinder radials or three 1,030bhp (768kw) Fiat A.80 RC 41 radials.<br>SM84: three 850bhp (634kw) Alfa Romeo 128 engines or three 1,000bhp (746kw) Piaggio P.XI radials. |
| Performance: | SM79 maximum speed 267mph (430km/h) at 13,120ft (4,000m). Initial climb 1,100ft (335m) per min.<br>Service ceiling 21,325ft (6,500m).<br>Normal range 1,180 miles (1,898km). |
| Armament: | Maximum bomb load 2,755lb (1,250kg) or two 18" (45cm) torpedoes.<br>One 12.7mm machine gun in each of the cockpit, dorsal and ventral positions.<br>One 7.7mm machine gun in beam position. |

## Reggiane RE 2001

| | |
|---|---|
| Type: | Italian-built single-seat fighter. |
| Powerplant: | One 1,175bhp (876kw) Alfa Romeo RA 1000 RC 41 (license built Daimler Benz DB 601) inverted V12. |
| Performance: | Maximum speed 339mph (545km/h) at 17,945ft (5,470m).<br>Service ceiling 36,090ft (11,000m).<br>Range 684 miles. |

149

| Armament: | Two 12.7mm machine guns in the nose.<br>Two 7.7mm machine guns or 20mm cannon in wings.<br>Capable of carrying one 1,410lb (640kg) bomb under fuselage. |

### Macchi MC 202

| Type: | Italian-built single-seat fighter. |
| Powerplant: | One 1175bhp (876kw) Alfa Romeo RA 1000 RC 41-1 Monsone (license-built Daimler-Benz DB 601A) inverted V12. |
| Performance: | Maximum speed 372mph (598km/h) at 18,370ft (5,600m).<br>Service ceiling 37,730ft (11,500m).<br>Normal range 475 miles (764m). |
| Armament: | Two 12.7mm machine guns in the nose.<br>Some later aircraft were fitted with an additional two 7.7mm machine guns in the wings, or two 20mm cannon under the wings. |

### Messerschmitt Bf 109F

| Type: | German-built single-seat fighter-bomber. |
| Powerplant: | One 1,350bhp (1,007kw) Daimler Benz DB 601E-1 inverted V12. |
| Performance: | Maximum speed 390mph (628km/h) at 21,980ft (6,700m).<br>Maximum speed at sea level 334mph (537km/h).<br>Service ceiling 39,370ft (12,000m).<br>Range with drop tank 528 miles (850km). |
| Armament: | One 20mm cannon.<br>Two 7.9mm machine guns. |

'B' derivative provision for one 551lb (250kg) bomb under the fuselage.

## Notes

[1]  *AIRCRAFT OF WWII*, Stewart Wilson, Aerospace Publications, 1998, except where otherwise stated.

[2]  *BRITISH WARPLANES OF WORLD WAR II*, ed. Daniel J. March, Grange Books, 2000, p. 160.

# Select Bibliography

Bragadin, Commander (Ret.) Marc' Antonio, (1957), *The Italian Navy in World War II*, United States Naval Institute.

Cameron, Ian, (1959), *Red Duster, White Ensign, The Story of the Malta Convoys*, Frederick Muller Ltd.

Douglas-Hamilton, James, (2000), *The Air Battle for Malta*, Airlife Publishing Ltd.

Hill, Lieutenant Commander Roger, (1975), *Destroyer Captain*, Wm. Kimber & Co.

Hague, Arnold, (2000), *The Allied Convoy System 1939–1945*, Chatham Publishing.

Jenkins, Roy, (2001), *Churchill*, Macmillan.

Jordan, Roger, (1999), *The World's Merchant Fleets 1939*, Chatham Publishing.

Kesselring, Field-Marshal Albert, (1974), *The Memoirs of Field-Marshal Kesselring*, The Book Club, by arrangement with Wm. Kimber.

Lenton, H.T., (1998), *British and Empire Warships of the Second World War*, Greenhill Books, Lionel Leventhal Ltd.

March, Daniel J., (ed.), (2000), *British Warplanes of World War II*, Grange Books.

Mitchell, W.H. & Sawyer, L.A., (1990), *The Empire Ships*, Second Edition, Lloyds of London Press Ltd.

Murray, Williamson, (2000), *Strategy for Defeat, The Luftwaffe 1933–1945*, Eagle Editions Ltd.

Pimlott, Dr John (ed.), (1994), *Rommel in his own words*, Greenhill

Books, Lionel Leventhal Ltd.

Shankland, Peter & Hunter, Anthony, (1969), *Malta Convoy*, Fontana Books.

Slader, John, (1995), *The Fourth Service, Merchantmen at War 1939–45*, New Era Writers Guild.

Smith, Peter C., (1999), *Pedestal, The Convoy that saved Malta*, Crecy Publishing Ltd.

Spooner, Tony, (1996), *Supreme Gallantry, Malta's Role in the Allied Victory 1939–1945*, John Murray (Publishers) Ltd.

Toland, John, (1997), *Hitler*, Wordsworth Editions Ltd.

Wilson, Stewart, (1998), *Aircraft of WWII*, Aerospace Publications Ltd.

Woodman, Richard, (2000), *Malta Convoys*, John Murray (Publishers) Ltd.

# MALTA
## Strategic Crossroads of the Mediterranean

154

# The Maltese Archipelago

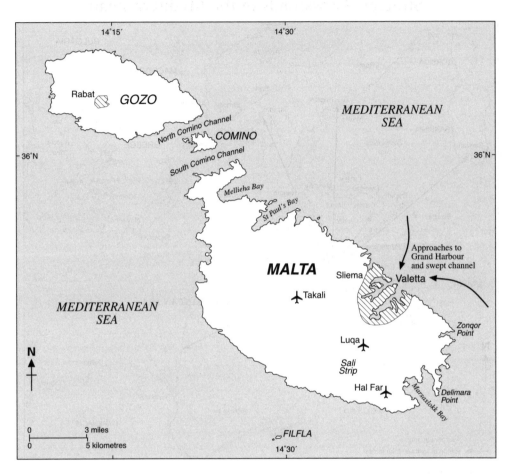

# The Voyage of the *Ohio*

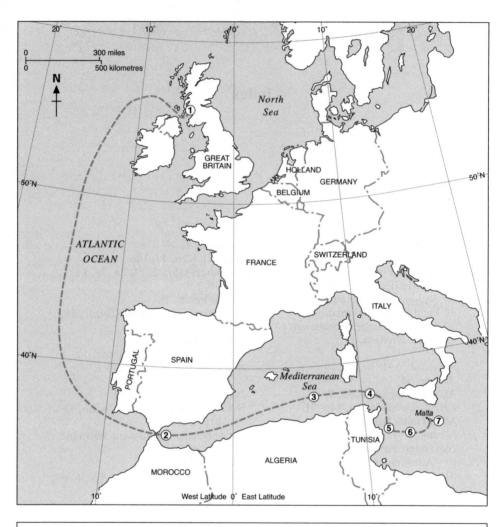

The voyage of the *Ohio*. Departing the Clyde 2 August she arrived Malta 15 August, 1942

(1) Sailed 2 August, 1942
(2) Straits of Gibraltar 9/10 August
(3) Commencement of air attack
(4) Torpedoed 12 August
(5) Numerous air attacks. Boilers wrecked, 13 August
(6) Rudder carried away by near-miss bomb blast, 14 August
(7) Towed in by warships, berthing 15 August, 1942

# Index

159

Mowatt, Lieutenant Commander G., RD, RNVR, 142
Mowlam, Lieutenant Commander J., 142
Murmansk, 27, 35
Murphy, Second Engineer James, 33, 40
Musham, Gunner Charles, 84, 97
*Muzio Attendolo*, 82, 83
Mussolini, Benito, 2, 3, 5, 15, 83

Naples, 8
Naval Fuelling Authority, 106
Nelson, Admiral Lord Horatio, 1
*Nelson*, HMS, 49, 57, 67, 139
Nelson, Lynn, 36
Nelson, W., 39
*Neptune*, HMS, 9
*Nigeria*, HMS, 46, 68, 71–2, 73, 140
Noble, Lieutenant Commander A. H., DSC, 140
Northey, Lieutenant A. P., DSC, 140

O'Connor, General Sir Richard, 3–4, 117
O'Mara, Danny, 95, 107–8
Official Secrets Act, 108
*Ohio*
  armament, 35, 36
  arrives in Malta, 104
  arrives in U.K., 32
  attempts to move, 98
  back on convoy, 84
  bombed, 91
  bonded store opened, 100
  captain, 41
  cargo, 115
  catches up with convoy, 81
  crew accommodation, 22
  crew lists, 127–132
  crew reboard ship, 90
  crew temporarily leave ship, 89–90
  damage from torpedo, 74
  damaged in bombing raid, 84
  design, 19–22
  details, 121–6
  difficulty in moving, 96
  equipment, 38, 40–1
  first cargo, 23

  first U.S. tanker in Britain after Pearl Harbor, 28
  gets under way after torpedo hit, 76
  gunners shoot down aircraft, 99
  hit by crashing aircraft, 87
  hit by torpedo, 70–1
  in bombing raid, 86
  launch, 19, 22–3
  loss of rudder, 101
  modifications, 45
  motor launches sent to assist, 89
  nickname, 39
  requisitioned from Texaco, 29
  salvage claim, 110
  sets sail for Malta, 47
  sinking, 120
  spots U-boat, 57
  taken in tow, 91–2
  transfers to British flag, 32–3
  trials, 23
  under attack, 60–2, 68–70
  volunteer crew, 97
  welcome in Malta, 109–10
*Omega*, 107
Onslow, Commander Richard G., DSO, 72, 140
*Operation Barbarossa*, 6
*Operation Berserk*, 139
*Operation Crusader*, 8, 9
*Operation Harpoon*, 24, 25, 27
*Operation Pedestal*, 34–5, 42, 49, 50, 51, 53, 54, 55, 56, 61, 82, 85, 107, 108, 109, 110, 112, 113, 115, 139
*Operation Torch*, 28, 115, 118
*Operation Vigorous*, 24, 26, 27
*Oriani*, 26
Osburn, Lieutenant Commander H., OBE, RNR, 142

P.A.C. (Parachute and Cable) rocket launchers, 35–6
Pantelleria, 1, 52, 73, 79, 81
Panzer Armee, 7, 8, 12, 15
Parlatorio Wharf, 104
Parlour, Junior Engineer, 108
Partington, Lieutenant Commander R. E., RD, RNR, 141
*Partridge*, HMS, 24, 25
*Pathfinder*, HMS, 79, 82, 141